THE FRANCIS E. FOWLER, JR. COLLECTION OF SILVER

Catalogue by Timothy B. Schroder

Essay by John F. Hayward
Edited and Expanded by Timothy B. Schroder

FOWLER MUSEUM OF CULTURAL HISTORY
UNIVERSITY OF CALIFORNIA, LOS ANGELES

Opposite title page, left to right, top to bottom:

FMCH X87.791.A. *(Cat. 75, page 68).*
FMCH X87.1033.A. *(Cat. 1, page 23).*
FMCH X87.995. *(Cat. 117, page 99).*
FMCH X87.961. *(Cat. 106, page 94).*
FMCH X87.1033.B. *(Cat. 1, page 23).*
FMCH X87.799. *(Not in Catalogue).*
FMCH X87.1033.A. *(Cat. 1, page 23).*
FMCH X87.1023.A. *(Cat. 53, page 56).*
FMCH X87.976.C. *(Cat. 103, page 92).*

Fowler Museum of Cultural History
University of California, Los Angeles
405 Hilgard Avenue
Los Angeles, California, USA 90024-1549

Printed and bound by Nissha Printing Co., Ltd., Kyoto, Japan.

Library of Congress Cataloging-in-Publication Data:

University of California, Los Angeles
Fowler Museum of Cultural History
    The Francis E. Fowler, Jr. Collection of Silver
Catalogue by Timothy B. Schroder; essay by John F. Hayward,
edited and expanded by Timothy B. Schroder.
        p. cm.
    Includes bibliographical references.
    ISBN 0-930741-19-6 (Hardbound)
    ISBN 0-930741-20-X (Softbound)
    1. Silverwork – Catalogs. 2. Fowler, Francis E., 1892-1975 – Art
collections – Catalogs. 3. Silverwork – Private collections – California –
Los Angeles – Catalogs. 4. Silverwork – California – Los Angeles –
Catalogs. 5. University of California, Los Angeles. Fowler Museum
of Cultural History – Catalogs. I. Schroder, Timothy. II. Hayward, J.F.
(John Forrest). III. Title.
NK103.F68U5 1991
739.2'3'07479494 – dc20   91-73419
                                                          CIP

CONTENTS

Detail of centerpiece. FMCH X87.806.

ACKNOWLEDGMENTS

This publication not only documents the donation of a major collection to the University of California, but also celebrates a major step forward in the progress of the Museum of Cultural History – the opening of a completely new facility to house the Museum. With the inaugural exhibitions in 1992 we officially changed our name to the Fowler Museum of Cultural History in honor of the significant contributions of Francis E. Fowler, III and Philip F. Fowler, Sr. to the Museum.

The Fowler Museum of Cultural History was founded in 1963 by then Chancellor Franklin D. Murphy as the Museum and Laboratories of Ethnic Arts and Technology. Its initial mandate was to consolidate, organize and preserve the widely varied non-Western collections spread throughout the different departments of the University. With that task finished, attention was turned to building the collections, a process that was launched with the spectacular acquisition of a major portion of the Sir Henry Wellcome Collection. This gift included over 30,000 objects spanning much of the globe. A name change to the Museum of Cultural History in 1971 reflected more accurately the broadening scope of the Museum's collections and programs.

For most of its nearly thirty-year history, the Museum's collections and operations were inadequately housed in thirty-five converted offices and classrooms in Haines Hall. With a substantial lead gift from the Fowler family, the Museum was able to launch a successful fund raising campaign that resulted in the construction of a 100,000 square foot, three story facility designed specifically for its special needs.

We are especially pleased that the Fowler family has also decided to place their impressive silver collection at the Museum. The collection will serve as a resource for a rich variety of University programs. We are privileged to share this with the UCLA community and the general public of Southern California. The Francis E. Fowler, Jr. Silver Gallery will be an enduring memorial, and we are extremely appreciative of the family's generosity.

We would also like to acknowledge the continuing support of Chancellor Charles E. Young. His commitment to the Museum has been unfailing and the new building would not have been realized without his strong leadership. Vice Chancellor Elwin V. Svenson has also been a major catalyst in the development of the new museum. The guidance he has provided during this process has been critical to its success.

The preparation of this volume and its accompanying exhibition was facilitated by three individuals. Timothy Schroder organized the collection, edited and expanded John Hayward's essay, and wrote catalogue entries. Glenn Wharton confronted the staggering task of conserving the silver for photography and exhibition. James Hamilton graciously juggled a variety of assignments that made everyone's job both easier and more enjoyable. We greatly appreciate all of their efforts.

Christopher B. Donnan   Doran H. Ross

Detail of spice plate. FMCH X87.1034.1. *(See also Cat. 4, page 28)*.

FOREWORD

The objects described in this catalogue have been selected from the Francis E. Fowler, Jr. collection of silver, the greater part of which was given to UCLA in 1983. In making this selection two criteria were applied: some objects were chosen on the grounds of their artistic merit, while others were included because of their relevance to the context of a museum of cultural history. The Fowler collection is particularly well suited to such a setting as its unusual diversity gives the visitor a rare insight into the full range of European goldsmiths' work, from ordinary domestic vessels and implements to the grandest works of art which were never intended for practical use.

This is not a catalogue raisonné. Entries are intended to provide only the most basic information on marks, inscriptions and heraldry. While a few generally unfamiliar terms are explained, no attempt has been made to research provenance or to give an account of objects in terms of their function, rarity, or historical importance. Most historical information is to be found in the essays, and the occasional brief notes appended to figure captions are intended to augment what is said in the text.

The text is based on a series of three articles by the late John F. Hayward, originally published in *The Connoisseur* in 1971 and reproduced here in edited form by kind permission of the National Magazine Company.

I am grateful to a number of friends and colleagues for assistance in the preparation of this little catalogue. In particular I should like to thank Dr. Christopher Donnan of the Fowler Museum of Cultural History for inviting me to be involved with the project and Mr. James Hamilton of the Fowler Foundation for his friendly cooperation at every stage. I am grateful to Peter Dewar for research into less easily identified coats of arms and to Eleanor Thompson for bringing information to my attention concerning Cat. 99.

Timothy B. Schroder

The Fowler family home in St. Louis, Missouri, c. 1890.

FRANCIS E. FOWLER, JR.

In 1983, thanks to a generous gift from the Francis E. Fowler, Jr. Foundation, the Museum of Cultural History fell heir to an extraordinary collection of silver that broadened the Museum's purview and gave it vital connections with ongoing scholarship at UCLA. Dealing with something so different from its usual ethnographic collections presented a challenge to the Museum. It soon became apparent, however, that the Fowler collection brought with it an abundance of cultural history. It was equally clear that this collection reflected the keen eye, expansive taste, and generous heart of the man who had collected it. His personal history, as recounted by his son, Francis III, has the flavor of a genuine American archetype, and imparts its own meanings to the silver he collected.

Born in 1892 to a prominent family in St. Louis, Missouri, Francis grew up under the strong influence of his father and grandfather. His father, Francis E. Fowler, Sr., had left the Fowler family home in Newburyport, Massachusetts, to come west as a young surveyor for the Missouri-Pacific Railroad. Ultimately he went into the insurance business and founded "Francis E. Fowler & Company," the first insurance agency west of the Mississippi. But he never stopped regaling his children with stories of his youth – of "parlays" with Indians and rough-and-tumble living on the Missouri frontier.

It was Francis's grandfather, Edwin Fowler, who awakened in him the passion for collecting. Edwin, an ardent traveler, returned from every journey with exotic items which he displayed in the cupola of the family homestead. There he would take his grandchildren to show them his treasures and tell traveler's tales. In the late 1890s Edwin took a trip around the world. A photograph shows him in India, riding atop an elephant like Passepartout. On return, he presented Francis with a Chinese scarf pin carved from a peach pit. That pin cast its spell; the result was a lifelong fascination with the mystery of objects.

Like his father and grandfather before him, Francis Jr. was by temperament a man of action with a zest for life and an inventive, enterprising mind. He attended St. Louis University but it bored him and he dropped out after a couple of years: his mind was restless and he found university life too confining. Instead, to make a living, he joined his father in the insurance business, but turned his most serious attention to mechanical things. He was mad for cars. He also loved tinkering and finding new ways to make things work, having the instincts of a natural-born inventor.

In 1914 Francis went to a party and fell in love. Emily Riddle was the daughter of a Kentucky tobacco-grower who kept a second home in St. Louis; Francis started taking her for rides in his car. At that era an automotive courtship had its perils: on one memorable outing the car's axle broke off. But the engagement survived, and Francis and Emily were married on April 29, 1915. The newlyweds settled in a big home at 63 Kingsbury Place. The house had a basement that ran the whole length of the house and this was Francis's haven, the place where he fiddled with things each evening after work.

Francis's first noteworthy invention, probably in the late teens or early '20s, was a water temperature gauge designed to go on the dashboard, where the driver would be able to see it, rather than on the hood of the car, which was the usual place. Francis patented his idea but sales were disappointing. Then in 1929 he was approached by General Motors. GM had come up with its own model of dashboard thermometer and was being sued by the Boyce Company, which also claimed patent rights. When GM learned that Francis Fowler actually held the earliest patent, the company proposed to buy and use Fowler's patent so as to discredit the claim of its rival. Francis agreed, and in gratitude GM gave him a 1930 Cadillac: their top-of-the-line, 4-door sedan.

Some years earlier, hearing great things about California, Francis had gone west by railroad to have a look. Now impelled by the brand new Cadillac, he drove his family – there were three boys by this time – all the way to the west coast for a visit. Francis III recalls the arduous drive, which took at least six days; the most grueling part was crossing the desert on a road made of wooden planks, held together by cables. But the family made it intact to La Jolla, and within weeks Francis had bought a house there. It was high on a hill overlooking the ocean, although not too close because he thought that would be unhealthy. Each summer thereafter, and sometimes for a while in mid-winter, the family would enjoy the change of climate.

In the meantime, Francis continued to invent things. For the automobile he invented an additive called anzine, an ancestor of what we now call ethyl, to enhance the performance of gasoline. In addition he dreamed up innovative approaches to crafting and selling insurance, some of which are only now being used by other companies. In the words of Francis III, "He was always ahead of his time."

But by far his most successful discovery – from a business point of view – was a secret recipe for smoothing out the rough edges of whiskey. Prohibition was ending and Francis had a radical idea. Since whiskey was harsh on the throat, why not add sugar and give it a smooth flavor to make it more appealing to the ladies? Francis III recalls spending many Sundays in the basement watching his father try vials

Edwin Fowler, grandfather of Francis Fowler, Jr. *(top left),* during his travels in India in the late 1890s.

of this and that, until he had mixed the perfect concoction. An unmemorable drink called Southern Comfort had gone bust during Prohibition. Researching it, Francis discovered that the owners had never registered a patent. He purchased the name, bottled his own formula, and thus was born the sweet whiskey we know as Southern Comfort.

Establishing the new company required strategy. To coax the public into trying the new product, he took out a series of full-page color magazine advertisements, featuring a bottle of Southern Comfort. The visual hook was the photograph of an object from Francis Fowler's art collection. In addition there was a tantalizing recipe made with a dollop of Southern Comfort. The message was clear: Southern Comfort was for people who could recognize fine art and knew how to eat and drink in style. Later the ads went national and were featured in magazines such as *Life, Coronet,* and *TV Guide.* By this time, however, the ads no longer featured an art object, but focused on the recipe.

Among the new drinks inspired by this ad campaign was something called the Missouri Mule, for which Francis had a special drinking mug created. Pursuing a fascination with cups, mugs, and tankards of all kinds he organized the Southern Comfort collection of drinking vessels, which traveled around the country on display for many years.

It was during the Second World War that Southern Comfort gained popularity, for it was a "ladies' drink" at a time when ladies were in charge. In the post war years sales declined. But then in the late 1960s it enjoyed a second and unexpected surge. Francis Fowler, heartened by the sudden boom, discovered that its new popularity with young people had to do with one of their cultural idols, flamboyant rock singer Janis Joplin. It seems that when Janis was in concert she had the habit of bringing along a bottle of Southern Comfort, and she would take a sip between songs to smooth her throat and ease her way through the stormy emotions of performance. As Francis III puts it, "Janis Joplin did more for us than any ad." Being a believer in the personal touch, Francis took it upon himself to thank Miss Joplin. He called her up and asked if there was anything she might desire. Yes, she replied, she would *love* a fur coat and new pair of high boots. Francis Fowler was happy to oblige, and had the items dispatched to her!

Part of the genius of the Southern Comfort business was its simplicity. Nothing was made at the factory: ingredients purchased elsewhere (whiskey, sugar, and flavorings) were merely assembled and bottled. Toward the end of World War II, while business was still booming, it occurred to Francis that he could supervise operations just as well from the west coast as from St. Louis. He purchased a house on Saltair Avenue from actor Fred MacMurray, and in 1944 moved his family to Los Angeles. In 1948 he had an office constructed in the center of Brentwood Village. The office structure was another manifestation of Fowler's original mind. Though intended purely as office space, it was built and furnished so as to look and feel like a private home. The main office had a fireplace and was appointed with fine antique furniture, art objects, and comfortable leather chairs. As Francis said, "Why shouldn't a person be as comfortable at work as at home?"

Francis E. Fowler, Jr. with some of his favorite drinking vessels.

Collecting came as naturally to Francis as breathing. His love affair with objects, begun in childhood, was unpretentious and wide-ranging; anything unusual, interesting, or beautiful engaged him. But he was not especially possessive, for he regarded himself as much keeper as owner, and was quoted as saying, "In this world you are just the custodian of what you have" (*California Living*, April 19, 1970, p. 12).

It was in the 1930s that Francis began accumulating silver. Throughout that decade and the following one, he gathered fine pieces, bit by bit, small and large. The break-up of the J.P. Morgan estate, in 1947, provided his first remarkable treasure. It was then that he acquired the apostle spoons, the Elizabethan plates, and the de Lamerie ewer and dish. These rare and precious items were to become the masterpieces of the Fowler collection.

A story told by his son is evidence of the extraordinary pleasure he took in these pieces. The date was April 31, 1965, Francis and Emily Fowler's 50th wedding anniversary. To celebrate that august occasion, the Fowlers held a feast for their extended family. First came the fine meal – probably roast beef and Yorkshire pudding, which were family favorites. Then the dessert ware was fetched from the vault: none other than the apostle spoons and the Elizabethan plates engraved with the Labors of Hercules. Dessert, soft and easy on the plates, was chocolate ice cream with Southern Comfort sauce, to be scooped up with 300-year-old spoons.

In 1968, to house objects collected over a period of fifty years and to make them available to the public, Francis established his own museum in Westwood. The Francis E. Fowler, Jr. Foundation Museum was open weekday afternoons from one to five p.m. Its location at 10884 Weyburn Avenue, across from the University, enabled him to share his enthusiasm with students, whose company he particularly enjoyed. The exhibitions displayed his unique and eclectic tastes. Paper weights were cheek by jowl with antique firearms; carvings of jade, ivory, and amber sat near antique banks, snuff boxes, rare coins, and, of course, silver. There was something for everyone.

Four years later, in 1972, the museum was moved to a larger site in Beverly Hills, on Wilshire Boulevard. The new building offered four or five times as much space for the Fowler collections, which were indeed extensive. The family also entertained hopes that the new location, being central, would bring more visitors than the Westwood one, tucked away on a side street. Ironically, however, this proved not to be the case, for in contrast to Weyburn Avenue, which was always peopled with students, Wilshire sustained little foot traffic, and drop-in visitors were rare. Francis missed the student visitors and their eager curiosity.

The next years brought some difficulties for Francis. A bad fall obliged him to take to a wheelchair. Inspired by Raymond Burr's television character, Ironside, he had a special van built to accommodate the chair and still managed to be quite active. But when a fire damaged their home, Francis and his wife had to move to a rented house while repairs were made. Thereafter, his health deteriorated, and in 1975, at the age of 83, Francis Fowler died. His wife survived him by only three months.

The Wilshire Boulevard museum stayed open for another decade under the supervision of Francis III, who had assumed directorship of the Fowler Foundation. It closed in 1983, when the collections were gifted to UCLA. The Fowler gift stipulated that all but the silver could be sold, and the proceeds used as seed money toward the building of a new on-campus museum which would house, among other things, the Fowler silver. A Sotheby's auction in 1986 brought the desired proceeds and enabled the start of the new building.

The permanent display of the Fowler silver at UCLA is particularly fitting because Francis E. Fowler, Jr. was a man who discovered, in collecting, a path to higher learning; and he hoped that others, like himself, would find the world in a spoon. We expect that this collection will engage scholars, enrich the wider community, and invite all to explore new avenues of cultural history.

Henrietta B. Cosentino

ENGLISH AND IRISH SILVER

The English silver in the collection was acquired over a long period. The late Mr. Francis Fowler started collecting shortly after his marriage in 1916, but the most important acquisitions were made in 1947 at the dispersal of the J. Pierpont Morgan collection. Numerically the collection is strongest in later examples, but the earliest pieces include some of the most important surviving Elizabethan silver. These are the twelve engraved and parcel-gilt spice or fruit plates, struck with the maker's mark of the hooded falcon and the London hallmark for 1567 (Cat. 4). Each plate is engraved in the central depression with one of the twelve Labors of Hercules, while the borders are decorated with medallion heads alternating with panels of foliage. The scenes of the Labors are adapted from the series engraved by Heinrich Aldegrever of Soest (1502-1555). The series is dated 1550 and so belongs to the last years of the master's working life. Three of the plates are signed with the engraver's monogram: the letters P over M.

These plates belong to a rare group of Elizabethan silver decorated entirely with engraving. Besides this set, three other sets of plates are known, as well as a ewer and dish. All date from a short period; the earliest are the Fowler plates and the ewer and dish (formerly Morgan Collection, now Museum of Fine Arts, Boston) both from 1567; next a set of twelve from 1568 and 1569

Detail of engraved plate. FMCH X87.1034.D.
(See Cat. 4, page 27).

(Duke of Buccleuch collection); a set of six from 1573 (Victoria and Albert Museum); and finally another set of twelve in the Metropolitan Museum, unmarked but engraved by the same master P over M and apparently about the same date as the first set. The ewer and dish are engraved with Old Testament subjects based upon Bernard Salomon's illustrations to the Lyons Bible and with full-length and bust portraits of the English sovereigns from William the Conqueror to Queen Elizabeth I. The master of the monogram P over M has therefore left us quite a range of work, considering his early date. The problem of his identity has not yet been solved. His use of continental sources – Aldegrever and Salomon – has given rise to the suggestion that he was probably one of the many Protestant immigrants who came to England to escape persecution in the Low Countries. He did not, however, rely entirely on foreign sources, for he could hardly have found continental prints for the portraits of English kings and queens.

There is no doubt about the presence of numerous immigrant goldsmiths and other artists in London at that time; their competition led to protests from the native-born English goldsmiths. In 1575 and again in 1605 the London goldsmiths' company endeavored to restrict competition in future by prohibiting its members from accepting children of immigrants as apprentices.

The Fowler plates are believed to have belonged to Sir Richard Cotton (1571-1631) from whom they descended through the Earls of Denbigh until they were acquired by Mr. J. Pierpont Morgan. But in view of their date, Sir Richard cannot have been their first owner.

The original purpose of such plates is uncertain. Previous writers have used three different terms to describe them: fruit, dessert, or spice plates. The first two terms are modern and do not appear in contemporary inventories, whereas the 1574 inventory of the Jewels and Plate of Queen Elizabeth includes eighteen items described as "Spice-plates guilt." It also includes large numbers of "demi-platters" and of "sawsers." The latter can probably be excluded on the grounds that they seem to have been undecorated, but the demi-platters are described as being parcel-gilt and engraved. Unfortunately the inventory gives no indication of the character of the engraved ornament beyond referring to the presence of the "Queene's arms." It seems unlikely that even the most bored of inventory clerks could completely have ignored such fine engraving as that on the Fowler plates. The most likely suggestion is, therefore, that they were spice-plates, which were often elaborately decorated and stood on low feet. In addition to embossed or engraved ornament some were further embellished with glass or crystal plaques painted on the reverse with mythological or religious subjects. The royal spice-plates were indeed of such value that they were kept apart by the Sergeants of the Confectionery. A final point in favor of the spice-plate explanation is that those in the royal inventory seem to have come in sets of six, twelve, or eighteen, corresponding to the numbers of the three surviving English sets.

Details of apostle spoons. *(See Cat. 2, pages 24,25).* THIS PAGE: FMCH X87.1035.A. The Master. OPPOSITE: FMCH X87.1035.K. St. James the Greater.

These plates date from a period when it was customary to display such silver on a cupboard or buffet. In the more refined circles a sophisticated pleasure was taken in articles of domestic type that were made of such precious material as to be unsuitable for practical use. Contemporary engravings of subjects such as the feast of Nebuchadnezzar, the feast of Cana, and Christ supping at Emmaus often show great displays of plate including large numbers of dishes set vertically on edge against a tiered cupboard; and the Fowler set may have once been shown in this way.

Next in date of the Fowler silver are two of the "decent communion cuppes provided and kept for that purpose" (Cat. 11 and 12) of the type prescribed by Archbishop Parker after his appointment to the See of Canterbury, to replace the medieval chalices that had continued in use after Henry VIII's reformation of the church. The appearance of the English communion cup was due entirely to the liturgical consequences of the Reformation. In the Roman Liturgy the chalice was restricted to the celebrant priest, only the bread being taken by the congregation. Therefore, in most cases, the bowl of the chalice was small. In 1548, after the death of Henry VIII, the cup was made available to the laity. Although this was halted during the reign of Mary (1553-1558), when the country returned to Roman Catholicism, it was restored in 1559 following the succession of Elizabeth I. Steps were taken in 1548 and again after 1559 to convert the chalices into vessels of larger capacity. The intention seems to have been both practical and political: to produce a cup not only better suited to the new liturgy but also quite distinct in form from those of the old order. The replacement of chalices by communion cups took a considerable time to complete, but most of the very large number of Elizabethan communion cups extant – many of which are still in use – date from the years between 1565 and 1575. The two in the Fowler collection date from 1569 and 1571 respectively. The earlier example has a bowl of unusually tall form, while the later one corresponds to the standard Elizabethan type.

The second major acquisition from the Morgan collection was the set of twelve apostle spoons together with the Master spoon dating from 1617 (Cat. 2), all made by the same maker, who used the mark of a crescent enclosing a mullet. This set was formerly preserved in Swettenham Hall, Cheshire, and like the Elizabethan plates is of such rarity and great value that it falls outside the range of the modern collector. Sets of spoons with finials modeled as apostles were made in England from at least the fifteenth century. These sets were commonly divided among the beneficiaries of wills and would, like other plate, have been subject to the threat of the melting pot. Consequently very few such sets survive intact. The Fowler spoons are predated by only four complete, or nearly complete, sets. The earliest of all, also now in a Californian collection, is the 1527 set at the Huntington Library in Pasadena. Next in date is the 1536 set, formerly in the Astor collection at Hever Castle, and now in the British Museum; it is unique in replacing the figure of Christ with that of the Virgin. The only other sets to predate this are the Bernal set of 1539, which numbers eleven, and the set of twelve dating from 1566, which was presented by Archbishop Parker to Corpus Christi College, Cambridge, and still belongs to that institution.

The reign of Charles I is represented by one of the small dishes, known sometimes as saucers or sweetmeat dishes, sometimes as wine-tasters, of which a surprisingly large number survive. This particular example (Cat. 14) is more substantial than such pieces usually are, but one must concede that it represents a sad decline in quality in comparison with the Elizabe-

than parcel-gilt dishes. A further indication of the lowering of standards is the fact that the heraldic shield in the center is misplaced in relation to the two shell handles. It is difficult to explain why these small Charles I dishes should have survived with greater frequency than more important vessels of the same period. Possibly they were spared on account of their light weight, which meant that they did not contain enough precious metals to justify the operation of melting them.

Among the silver of the second half of the seventeenth century is a representative group of the two-handled drinking cups that were then so popular. The earlier examples are embossed, often in a somewhat rough and ready way, with floral designs of Dutch and French inspiration. The type is usually, and rightly, associated with the Restoration period, but the Fowler collection does include one Commonwealth example of 1658 (Cat. 16), showing that the return to fashion of decoration was not exclusively due to the change in political circumstances that followed upon the restoration of the monarchy in England. Other examples of baroque decoration on Commonwealth silver are in fact known, including a 1658 ginger jar, of the type that in sets of three and five constituted the most expensive and ostentatious chimney-piece decoration of the time. The Commonwealth cup is provided with what is sometimes described as a salver-cover; that is to say, the cover could be reversed and stood on the flat top of its finial. Presumably this was to make it possible to use the cover as a second drinking cup. In this case it is too small in circumference to serve as a stand for the cup – as was done in the case of the true salver-cover. A very similar cup of 1664 (Cat. 13) is of unusually small size, though at the time it was evidently considered large enough to make an adequate present. It has two sets of initials and the date 1672 on one side, recording the first gift, while on the base is a further inscription in early eighteenth-century lettering, accompanied by little flower sprays, reading "DONUM W * HAWKINS AD E * PARSONS."

The story of the great influence exerted by French immigrant Huguenot goldsmiths on the London trade has often been told (for example, see Schroder 1988b, pp. 139-76). The significance of the change effected by the Huguenots is well illustrated by a group of silver vessels in the Fowler collection wrought by London goldsmiths of native English birth, just about the time when Huguenot influence was beginning to make itself felt. The vessels are strikingly simple, made with the minimum of precious metal and in comparison with contemporary French wares, positively naive. The rarest is the little handle-less cup with saucer cover supported on three ball feet (Cat. 24). Made by Robert Cooper in 1695, it was probably intended to serve as a chocolate cup. It is of taller and more conical form than the usual silver teacup – if one can, in fact, apply the term usual at all to such rare vessels as silver teacups.

Another rare piece is the bulbous double cup (Cat. 18). This bears only a maker's mark and one would have been inclined to regard it as a provincial piece. But Jackson gives what appears to be a version of the same mark to a London master. Both these pieces have what one might call minimal decoration, namely a matted surface – in panels on the one and punched all over on the other. This type of ornament was popular in England during the middle decades of the seventeenth century and for a longer period in Germany and Central Europe, but it soon gave way to the infinitely more sophisticated Huguenot decoration. Even the monteith of 1693 (Cat. 22), which bears the mark of George Garthorne,

Detail of monteith. FMCH x87.819. *(See Cat. 22, page 40).*

a maker who worked for the Royal Jewel Office, falls well below French standards; the cast cherubs' heads set at intervals around the rim have, for instance, the minimum chasing and much of their surface is still rough from the sand mold.

It would not, however, be correct to suggest that the Fowler collection lacks fine examples of the work of English-born goldsmiths of the Huguenot era. Catalogue number 28, for example, is a superb hexafoil dish of 1722, of a type that was done nowhere better than in England. The maker's mark is that of Anthony Nelme, who was one of the most successful English-born goldsmiths in competing with the Huguenots – though it has been suggested that his success may have been achieved by his employing them in his workshop. Another successful English maker was Gabriel Sleath, represented here by the chocolate pot in lighthouse form of 1716 (Cat. 30). A typically English piece, this pot well illustrates the excellence of early Georgian design. The contrast in form between the curved spout and the tall conical body is a particularly pleasing feature.

The earlier Huguenot masters are not well represented in the Fowler collection, but the beginning of a new style can already be recognized in the tulip-shaped beaker by Simon Pantin (Cat. 25). This has no date letter but is of Britannia standard and can therefore be ascribed to the period between 1704, when Pantin entered his mark, and 1719, when sterling standard was reintroduced.

There was a high degree of commercial cooperation between the leading Huguenot workshops in London. Extremely similar decoration that would appear to have been made from the same casting patterns is often found on pieces of virtually identical design but struck respectively with several makers' marks (cf. Cat. 1 and Schroder 1988a, cat. 47, fig. 52; also 1988b, pp. 189-90). In terms of quality these pieces are indistinguishable and most likely they were all produced in a single workshop and supplied to the others on a subcontracting basis.

The most spectacular pieces in the Fowler collection are the huge silver-gilt ewer and companion sideboard dish made in 1726 and bearing the mark of Paul de Lamerie (Cat. 1). Like so much of de Lamerie's work they are of Britannia standard silver (95.8% pure), in spite of the fact that sterling (92.5%) had been re-introduced as a legal alloy for plate seven years before. The precise reason for his continuing to use Britannia standard metal is not known; presumably he found some technical advantage in the softer material. It seems unlikely that his customers specified its use, as it would merely have brought them greater expense without any visible advantage. Study of these two pieces justifies the high regard accorded to de Lamerie as a goldsmith; the chasing of the heads on the border of the dish and of the straps applied to the body of the ewer is of outstanding quality.

These vessels are generally known as the Anson ewer and dish, after George Anson (1697-1762), first Baron Litchfield, First Lord of the Admiralty, whose arms they bear. The arms are cast separately and applied to both ewer and dish and this cannot have been done until after his marriage to Lady Elizabeth York in 1748. It is interesting to speculate just when the ewer and dish were first acquired by Anson. He had a successful career as a naval officer, but it was not until the year 1743, when a ship under his command captured a Spanish galleon bound from Manila to Acapulco, carrying treasure to the value of over half a million pounds in bullion, that he was in a position to acquire major pieces

Detail of the Anson dish. FMCH X87.1033.B. *(See Cat. 1, page 23).*

of plate. Such was the jubilation over the prize that the bullion, after landing at Portsmouth in 1744, was sent up to London and paraded through the City in a procession of thirty-two wagons, the ship's company marching and the band playing. In view of the long period that elapsed between the hallmarking of the ewer and dish and their acquisition by Anson – not less than eighteen years – it seems quite likely that he bought them second-hand. Although de Lamerie was still working when the arms were added, we cannot be certain that he was responsible for making them. The probability is, however, in his favor, as Lord Anson made other purchases from him about this time, including four dessert dishes of 1746 which are also in the Fowler collection (Cat. 40).

It is curious that when the armorial cartouche was cast to fit the ewer it was made very slightly too large and it overlaps the molded surround above and below. When de Lamerie was commissioned to make a ewer with coat of arms in relief he preferred to model them in one with the body of the ewer, as he has done in the case of the ewer of the Worshipful Company of Goldsmiths of 1741, as well as that made for the Earl of Mountrath of 1742, now in the Los Angeles County Museum of Art. Although both ewer and dish date from the same year, there is no obvious connection between their ornament, but this was probably of little consequence as they were sideboard pieces intended to be seen from a distance. Their combined weight is 485 oz. 8 dwt., a vast quantity of precious metal, but no great matter for a man who had captured a Spanish treasure galleon.

This ewer and dish represent the very highest level of de Lamerie's achievement. His more average production is also represented in the collection by two fine tea caddies of 1731

(Cat. 5) which are engraved with the arms of Sir William Johnstone of Westerhall, Dumfriesshire. One of de Lamerie's many claims to fame is the fact that he seems to have been the first to apply asymmetrical rococo ornament to silver in England. The asymmetrical detail appears at first in a very modest form – just an engraved scroll turning away instead of towards its companion scroll on the other side of a cartouche. His earliest use, as far as we know, dates from the year 1731. That is in fact the year of these tea caddies, on which asymmetrical detail can be found in the engraved borders on the top. At this date, however, most English goldsmiths still favored the symmetrical style of decoration illustrated by the attractive little bullet teapot of 1732 by Gabriel Sleath (Cat. 32).

Even fifteen years later some makers continued to resist the new rococo fashion and adhered to the simpler forms of the early Georgian style, when the new fashion was firmly established throughout western Europe. An example of this conservative approach is the handsome coffee pot of 1747 by William Grundy (Cat. 42). The only concession to current fashion is the slightly asymmetrical form of the scroll below the spout. Conversely, the makers of the fine tureen and its companion stand (Cat. 3) showed the fullest sympathy with and understanding of the rococo. In producing the tureen of 1756, Edward Wakelin, who took over the business of George Wickes, goldsmith to the Prince of Wales, showed awareness of contemporary French fashion, which can be recognized in the spiral fluting of the body and cover in the naturalistic pomegranate finial. The stand for the tureen was made some years later by Wakelin when in

De Lamerie tea caddy, showing slightly asymmetrical detail. FMCH X87.863. *(See Cat. 5, page 30).*

partnership with John Parker. The few pattern books of silver published in England about the middle of the eighteenth century were, curiously enough, the work of furniture designers, such as John Linnell or Thomas Johnson, and show little of the feeling for silver achieved by the designer of this tureen. The designs of Juste-Aurèle Meissonnier and Thomas Germain were current in England as well as in France and it is probably to some continental source that this tureen owes its excellent form. Despite its apparent frivolity it has the solidity of all good English silver, weighing over 130 ounces.

The Fowler collection includes one of the finest extant pieces of Irish Georgian silver, the large wine fountain (Cat. 7) by Robert Calderwood bearing Dublin hallmarks for 1754. This is of great interest not only on account of its handsome design but also of its rarity. A number of English wine fountains have survived, mostly dating from the first quarter of the eighteenth century, but this appears to be the only example of its type; that is, with a flat back enabling it to be hung on a hook on the wall. Its construction corresponds to the continental type of appliance usually found in pottery, porcelain, or pewter. The latter was accompanied by a basin below and was intended for washing. It seems hardly conceivable that the Irish nobleman for whom it was made would have used so magnificent a vessel for ablutions and I am inclined to accept the view that it was intended for wine. This is supported by the fact that, unlike the wall water fountains, it has a flat bottom so that it could also be stood on a side table. Nevertheless the possibility cannot entirely be excluded that it was once a luxurious piece of bathroom furniture.

Although it is struck with the Dublin hallmark for 1754, it bears the coat of arms of Fitzgerald impaling O'Brien for Robert, 19th Earl of Kildare and his wife, Mary, daughter of the third Earl of Inchiquin. The Earl of Kildare died in 1744, ten years before the cistern was hallmarked, and the marriage took place even earlier, in 1709. It seems, therefore, that it must actually have been made for his son, James Fitzgerald, 20th Earl of Kildare. This nobleman had a highly successful career in Ireland and, after being advanced first to an English viscounty, went on to an Irish marquisate, an English earldom and finally the Irish dukedom of Leinster. The fountain presents a curious problem – namely the use of the arms of the 19th earl and his wife by his son, ten years after the former's death. There appear to be three possible explanations: first, that the wine fountain was ordered by the father and not delivered until ten years later; second, that the coat of arms was removed from another piece and re-used – perhaps for sentimental reasons, when the new fountain was made; or, third, and perhaps most probably, that the fountain was made as a specific bequest from father to son and therefore engraved with the arms of the former.

The fountain is surmounted by an earl's coronet and the spigot on the tap is modeled as a monkey – one of the supporters of the Fitzgerald coat. At first sight it looks old-fashioned for the date at which it was made. But its design is somewhat of a compromise, the plain gadrooned mold-

ings looking back to the early Georgian period, while the dropped bottom of the body and the asymmetrical escutcheon over the arms are typical of the third quarter of the century. The weight (181 oz. 15 dwt.), which is inscribed on the back, is substantial but not vast by comparison with the few surviving English wine fountains.

The Regency period and in particular the works of Paul Storr have greatly interested American collectors in recent years; and as one might expect, the works of the leading London goldsmiths of the early nineteenth century are well represented in the Fowler collection. The names most frequently encountered are those of Paul Storr and of Digby Scott and Benjamin Smith, but although the pieces themselves bear the marks of one or other of these makers, they were mostly commissioned by the retail firm Rundell, Bridge and Rundell, which in the early years of the century enjoyed almost a monopoly of major orders. It is not known exactly when Storr first began to work exclusively for Rundell and Bridge, but it was probably about 1800, the year of the sauce tureen (Cat. 68). Storr completed his apprenticeship and became "free," or a full member, of the goldsmiths' company in 1792 and his earliest works are in the neoclassical style. This sauce tureen still follows the neoclassical style, but in some details, in particular the fleshy waterlily leaves, the heavier manner of the nascent Regency can be recognized. The Regency had its moments of serious archaeology and the coffee pot of 1812 (Cat. 81), also by Storr, illustrates such a moment. Ornament is confined to the gadrooned molding at the top of the body and the anthemion on the underside of the spout, while the plain body is based on a classical bronze. The ivory inserts in the handle are probably later additions. This type of coffee pot was often accompanied by a lamp and stand.

The collection is particularly rich in tankards, of English, Irish, and continental origin, and dating from the mid-seventeenth century to the early nineteenth. These include many examples in original condition, such as a rare Dublin tankard of 1685 (Cat. 19), but also others that illustrate the alterations to which tankards in particular were subjected during the Victorian era – added embossing, conversion for use as a jug by the addition of a spout, and so on. One of the

Detail of wine fountain spigot. FMCH X87.1032. *(See Cat. 7, page 31).*

most handsome is undoubtedly the Regency tankard (Cat. 90) of 1815 by William Elliot. Though following traditional lines, the goldsmith has given it the solid sturdy character of Regency plate and embellished it with a finely finished vine and grape girdle.

The most problematic pieces in the Fowler collection are the twelve silver-gilt cups and covers (Cat. 88) in three slightly variant patterns, represented by one, four, and seven cups respectively. At first sight they might be taken for mid-eighteenth-century cups in the rococo style, and this impression seems to be confirmed by the inscription engraved on four of the set: "The Gift of the Duke of Sussex to the Earl of Warwick 1760." The arms of the duke are engraved on one side and those of the earl on the other of each of the four. There are, however, certain difficulties in accepting this statement at its face value, since the Duke of Sussex, ninth son of George III and a notable collector of antique silver, was not born until 1773. The other eight cups from the set of twelve have the arms of the Duke of Sussex on an escutcheon on the foot, the escutcheon on the opposite side being blank. Seven of the eight have the wording "HRH Duke of Sussex" inscribed around the cover.

None of the cups bears a hallmark, but there is clear evidence on each that the original marks have been polished out at the same spot under the lip. There are two possible reasons for the removal of the marks: either they were not genuine, or they did not correspond to the date 1760 which had been added to four of them. In fact, the form of the cups recalls the revived rococo of the 1830s and 1840s rather than that of 1760 and there is little doubt that these cups are the work of Paul Storr, or perhaps castings from originals by Storr. Another cup of the same design has been recorded; it is struck with the maker's mark of Storr and the London hallmarks for 1837. It bears, moreover, the cypher of Queen Victoria and the initials of Lady Victoria Elizabeth Ashley and was given as a christening present by the Queen to the child who was born in 1837. The fact that the design was used as a christening present may explain the existence of so many as twelve cups of more or less the same design in the possession of the Duke of Sussex. He may have needed to provide such christening presents in quantity and have laid in a sufficient stock for a philoprogenitive age. Here again there is a difficulty, as the presence of so many cups together must mean that they were never presented to godchildren. In that case the cups should have appeared in the collection of the duke when he died in 1843. His collection was sold at Christie's in a series of four sales in June 1843; in all, over 40,000 ounces were disposed of. Like others of the period, the catalogues do not give much information about the individual pieces, but the descriptions are sufficiently detailed for the cups to be recognizable. They are not found in the catalogues, and if any of them had belonged to the duke they must have passed out of his possession before his death.

If the detail of the engraving on the cups is examined under magnification it proves to be far from clear, and it seems at least possible that the cups are not originals but castings from three originals. This would explain the existence of so many cups of a very similar design. Although he was a keen collector, the Duke of Sussex would hardly have wanted to crowd his sideboard with twelve presentation cups. This theory would also explain why the marks were removed subsequently – namely, in order to conform to the English regulations enforced by the Worshipful Company of Goldsmiths. Nevertheless, the possibility cannot be excluded that the cups themselves are genuine works of Paul Storr, perhaps made for stock for eventual use as christening cups, and that only the inscriptions are irregular.

Detail of tureen finial. FMCH X87.873. *(See Cat. 3, page 26).*

1. EWER AND DISH. Silver-gilt.

Marks: London, Britannia standard, 1726-27, maker's mark of Paul de Lamerie (Grimwade no. 1892); marked on reverse of border of dish and on lip of ewer.

Heraldry: The arms are those of Anson quartering Carrier and impaling Yorke, for Admiral George Anson (1697-1762), Baron Anson of Soberton, who in 1748 married Lady Elizabeth Yorke, daughter of the Lord Chancellor, Philip, Earl of Hardwick. Anson gained fame for his circumnavigation of the globe in 1740-44. During that voyage he captured a Spanish galleon carrying bullion worth £500,000. He was raised to the peerage in 1747.

A number of very similar pieces with different makers' marks are known, in particular an almost identical ewer and dish of the same year with the maker's mark of David Willaume (see Schroder 1988a, fig. 52).

Height of ewer: 37cm (14½"). **Diameter of dish:** 67cm (26⅛").

FMCH X87.1033.A,B. *See text, page 19.*

23

2. THIRTEEN APOSTLE SPOONS.
Silver, parcel-gilt.

Marks: London, sterling standard, 1617-18, maker's mark a crescent enclosing a mullet (Jackson p.115).

Length: 17.5 to 18.5 cm (6¾" to 7¼").

FMCH X87.1035.A-M.

See text, page 17.

LEFT TO RIGHT:

St. Matthias
St. Thomas
St. James the Less
St. John
St. Simon Zelotes
St. Matthew
The Master
St. Philip
St. Bartholemew
St. Jude
St. James the Greater
St. Andrew
St. Peter

3. SOUP TUREEN AND STAND. Silver.

Marks: London, sterling standard, 1756-57, maker's mark of Edward Wakelin (Grimwade no. 656); the stand with maker's mark of John Parker and Edward Wakelin (Grimwade no. 1602); the tureen marked under the base, the stand and cover part marked.

Heraldry: The crest is unidentified.

This tureen and stand is evidently from a set or a dinner service which was supplied over several years and the various parts of which were subsequently muddled up. The tureen is engraved "No. 1" and the stand "No. 2." Moreover, while the tureen is fully marked for 1756, the stand, which has no date letter, is struck with the Parker and Wakelin maker's mark which does not seem to have been registered until after 1758.

Width: 39 cm (15¼"). FMCH X87.873.A-C. *See text, page 20.*

4. TWELVE PLATES. Silver, parcel-gilt.

Marks: London, sterling standard, 1567-68, maker's mark a falcon (Jackson p. 101); each marked under rim. Three plates additionally signed by the unidentified engraver, P over M.

Diameter: 19.8 cm (7¾"). FMCH X87.1034.A-L.

See text, pages 15 and 16.

Literature: Clayton 1985, p. 275, pl. 402; Oman 1978, pp. 37-46, 141-6.

OPPOSITE PAGE: A B
C D

FOLLOWING PAGES: E F G H
I J K L

5. TWO TEA CADDIES. Silver.

Marks: London, sterling standard, 1731-32, maker's mark of Paul de Lamerie (Grimwade no. 1892); each marked under the base, the cover with lion passant only, the maker's mark apparently overstriking the same goldsmith's Britannia standard mark (LA).

Heraldry: The arms are those of Johnstone, probably for Sir William Johnstone of Westerhall, Dumphriesshire. The cover of the larger caddy is engraved with the Johnstone crest and the smaller with initials GJ.

These caddies presumably originally belonged to a set of three, the third of which would have made a pair with the smaller of the two shown.

Height: 13.5 cm (5¼").

FMCH X87.862.A,B, and FMCH X87.863.A,B.

See text, page 20.

6. (BELOW LEFT).
PAIR OF CADDIES AND A SUGAR BOX.
Silver.

Marks: London, sterling standard, 1747-48, maker's mark of Samuel Taylor (Grimwade no. 2645); the sugar box marked under base, part marked on cover; the caddies part marked on the sliding base.

Heraldry: The arms are those of Gold of Alarston, Wiltshire, possibly impaling Hawes of London.

The set is contained in a contemporary Chinese carved and pieced ivory case with unmarked English silver mounts.

Height of ivory case: 15.3 cm (5¾").

FMCH X87.1020.A-I.

7. WINE FOUNTAIN. Silver.

Marks: Dublin, 1754-55, maker's mark of Robert Calderwood (Jackson p. 612); marked on lip, part marked on cover.

Heraldry: The arms are those of Fitzgerald impaling O'Brien, for Robert, 19th Earl of Kildare (1675-1744), who in 1709 married Mary, first daughter of William, 3rd Earl of Inchiquin. He succeeded his father to the title in 1707. The countess died in 1780, aged 88, and it is possible that this fountain, made some ten years after the death of the earl, was commissioned for the use of his widow.

Height: 57 cm (22¼"). FMCH X87.1032.A-C.

See text, pages 20 and 21, for alternative explanations for the presence of the 19th earl's coat of arms.

8. CENTERPIECE. Silver.

Marks: London, sterling standard, 1816-17, maker's mark of Paul Storr (Grimwade no. 2234); marked on central basket, part marked on branches, nozzles and under base of stand.

Height: 46.3cm (18").

Width: 52.5cm (20½").

FMCH X87.804.A-Q.

9. PAIR OF WINE COOLERS. Silver.

Marks: London, sterling standard, 1813-14, maker's mark of Paul Storr (Grimwade no. 2234); each marked on side, part marked on liners and collars. Also signed "Rundell Bridge et Rundell, Aurifices Regis et Principis Walliae Regentis Britannias."

Heraldry: The arms are those of Agar quartering Ellis, for Welbore Ellis Agar, second Earl of Normanton (1778-1868), who succeeded his father in 1809 and in 1816 married Diana, daughter of George Augustus, 11th Earl of Pembroke. The Ellis quartering is in reference to the earl's paternal grandmother, Anne, only daughter of the Right Hon. and Right Rev. Welbore Ellis, Bishop of Meath. The Latin signature is for the retailers and is translated "Rundell, Bridge and Rundell, Goldsmiths to the King and to the Prince of Wales, Regent of Britain." These two coolers are stamped 1 and 4 and therefore originally belonged to a larger set.

Height: 28.4cm (11"). **Width:** 31.5cm (12¼").

FMCH X87.856.A-F.

10. DRINKING HORN. Silver-gilt and ivory.

Marks: London, sterling standard, 1813-14, maker's mark of Thomas Phipps, James Phipps II and Edward Robinson (Grimwade no. 2892); part marked on all parts.

The inscription running around the lip is in Gaelic and translates "Peace and Plenty." In general form, if not in detail, this is a revival of a medieval drinking vessel, the body of which would probably have been made of horn rather than ivory. It was presumably made for a special presentation in Ireland, although the circumstances of the commission are not known.

Height: 67 cm (26⅛"). FMCH X87.1027.A-D.

11. (ABOVE, LEFT). **COMMUNION CUP.** Silver.

Marks: London, sterling standard, 1568-69, maker's mark an orb and cross (Jackson p. 101); marked on lip.

Height: 17.2 cm (6¾"). FMCH X87.813. *See text, page 16.*

12. (ABOVE, RIGHT). **COMMUNION CUP.** Silver.

Marks: London, sterling standard, 1571-72, maker's mark TEo in monogram (Jackson p. 101); marked on lip.

Height: 16.7 cm (6½"). FMCH X87.814. *See text, page 16.*

13. PORRINGER. Silver.

Marks: London, sterling standard, 1664-65, maker's mark IR (Jackson p. 132); marked under base. The porringer is pricked beneath the lip with date and initials EI over EB between 16 and 72 and is engraved under the base DONUM W*HAWKINS AD E*PARSONS.

Height: 6.9 cm (2¾"). FMCH X87.823.

See text, page 17.

14. SAUCER. Silver.

Marks: London, sterling standard, 1634-35, maker's mark HS over a star (Jackson p. 117).

Width: 5 cm (1"). FMCH X87.825.

See text, page 17.

15. PEG TANKARD. Silver.

Marks: York, 1673-74, maker's mark of John Plummer (Jackson p. 289); marked on lip and part marked on cover.
The body of the tankard is engraved with initials M over RH. The term "peg tankard" refers to the five pegs, or studs, arranged vertically on the inside wall of the tankard and designed to divide the contents into fixed measures.

Height: 17cm (6⅝"). FMCH X87.800.

16. PORRINGER AND COVER. Silver.

Marks: London, sterling standard, 1658-59, maker's mark TG in dotted surround (Jackson p. 126); marked under base and on cover.

Height: 12.2cm (4¾").

FMCH X87.822.A,B. *See text, page 17.*

17. **TANKARD.** Silver.

Marks: London, sterling standard, 1681-82, maker's mark of Francis Garthorne (Jackson p. 138); marked on the lip and cover, the handle with maker's mark only. The embossed wreath on the front of the tankard is probably a later addition.

Height: 20.8cm (8⅛"). FMCH X87.798.

18. **DOUBLE BEAKER.** Silver. c. 1680.

Marks: Maker's mark only, IN (Jackson p. 148); marked under base of each, twice on one and once on the other.

Assembled height: 14cm (5½").

Individual height: 7.5cm (3").

FMCH X87.829.A,B. *See text, page 18.*

19. TANKARD. Silver.

Marks: Dublin, probably 1685-86, maker's mark GC (unrecorded by Jackson); marked on lip, maker's mark only on flange of cover.

Height: 18.6cm (7¼"). FMCH X87.928.

20. (LEFT). **TUMBLER CUP.** Silver.

Marks: London, sterling standard, 1684-85, maker's mark IP crowned (Jackson p. 137); marked under base.

Height: 5.7cm (2¼"). FMCH X87.827.

21. (RIGHT). **MUG.** Silver.

Marks: London, sterling standard, 1685-86, maker's mark overstruck by date letter; marked under base.

Height: 4.6cm (1¾"). FMCH X87.828.

22. MONTEITH. Silver.

Marks: London, sterling standard, 1693-94, maker's mark of George Garthorne (Jackson p. 148); marked under base, lion passant only on handles.

Heraldry: The arms are probably those of Blackborne of Yorkshire and Lancashire impaling one another.

Height: 18 cm (6⅝"). **Diameter:** 30 cm (11¾"). FMCH x87.819.

See text, page 18.

23. (RIGHT). MUG. Silver.

Marks: London, Britannia standard, 1701-2, maker's mark of William Gamble (Grimwade no. 738); marked on rim.

Height: 9.5 cm (3¾"). FMCH x87.807.

24. (ABOVE, LEFT). **BEAKER AND COVER.** Silver.

Marks: London, sterling standard, 1695-96, maker's mark RC in monogram (Jackson, p. 146, attributed to Robert Cooper); marked under base, the cover unmarked.

Height: 9 cm (3½"). FMCH X87.826.A,B. *See text, page 18.*

25. (ABOVE, RIGHT). **BEAKER.** Silver. c. 1705-15.

Marks: London, Britannia standard, maker's mark of Simon Pantin (Grimwade no. 2124); marked under base, date letter apparently overstruck by maker's mark.

The beaker is engraved with initials MM over an unidentified crest, a bird's wing and under the base with further initials, IL. The arrangement of the hallmarks in a straight line under the base suggests that the beaker falls into a category of English plate known as "duty dodgers." The makers of such objects cleverly avoided the duty payable on hallmarked plate by cutting the marks from a recently assayed piece and inserting the resulting patch into the new object, usually concealing the seam under the foot.

Height: 12.5 cm (4⅞"). FMCH X87.830. *See text, page 18.*

26. BOWL. Silver.

Marks: Dublin, 1699-1700, maker's mark of Thomas Boulton (Jackson p. 609); marked on rim.

Diameter: 28.6 cm (11⅛").

FMCH X87.929.

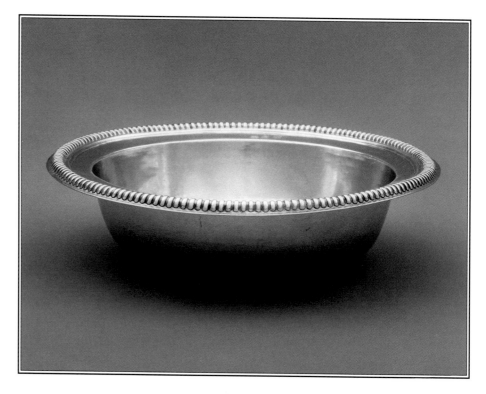

27. SALAD DISH. Silver.

Marks: London date letter for 1715-16, maker's mark illegible, London and Britannia standard marks missing and possibly removed; marked under base.

Heraldry: The dish is engraved with two coats of arms. The one in the center is slightly later than the dish and replaces other engraving that has been erased. The coat of arms on the outside of the dish is modern and is that of Bishop. The arms appear similar to those of Robinson, although the motto 'Essam quam videre' is not recorded as being used by any branch of that family.

Diameter: 21.6 cm (8½").

FMCH X87.879.

28. SALVER. Silver.

Marks: London, Britannia standard, 1722-23, maker's mark of Anthony Nelme (Grimwade no. 68); marked on salver, the feet each with lion's head only.

Heraldry: The arms are those of Tremwayne of Cornwall with another in pretence, probably Kemp of Ireland or Kempe of Norfolk.

Diameter: 32 cm (12½").

FMCH X87.836. *See text, page 18.*

29. SALVER. Silver.

Marks: London, sterling standard, 1739-40, maker's mark of James Shruder (Grimwade no. 1682); marked on reverse.

Heraldry: The arms in the 1st and 4th quarters are those of Williams of London. Those in the 2nd and 3rd quarters are unidentified.

Diameter: 49.3 cm (19¼").

FMCH X87.947.

30. CHOCOLATE POT. Silver and wood.

Marks: London, Britannia standard, 1716-17, maker's mark of Gabriel Sleath (Grimwade no. 2568 or 2569); marked on lip, the cover with lion's head only. Early eighteenth-century chocolate pots are identical in form to coffee pots and can be distinguished from the latter by a hinged finial which enables a stirrer to be inserted without lifting the cover.

Height: 22.3cm (8¾"). FMCH x87.832.

31. TWO DISHES. Silver.

Marks: Dublin, 1729-30, maker's mark of John Laughlin (Jackson p. 611); each marked under border.

Heraldry: The crest and ducal coronet are for Fitzgerald, probably for James Fitzgerald, Earl of Kildare (1722-73), who was elevated in 1766 to Duke of Leinster.

Although bearing hallmarks for 1729, the style of these dishes strongly suggests that their borders were altered at a later date. Such alterations were illegal, but were quite frequently carried out as they were cheaper than making completely new dishes. The Fowler dishes were probably altered in or after 1766, when the Earl of Kildare was created Duke of Leinster, to supplement the great dinner service supplied to him between 1745 and 1747 by George Wickes (see Barr pp. 197-205).

Diameter: 48.1 cm (18¾"). FMCH X87.935.

51 cm (20"). FMCH X87.936.

32. TEAPOT. Silver and wood.

Marks: London, sterling standard, 1732-33, maker's mark of Gabriel Sleath (Grimwade no. 890); marked under base, the cover with lion passant and maker's mark.

Length: 20 cm (8"). FMCH X87.834.

See text, page 20.

33. PAIR OF CANDLESTICKS. Silver.

Marks: London, sterling standard, 1732-33, maker's mark of James Gould (Grimwade no. 1317); each marked under base, the sockets with lion passant.

Height: 17 cm (6⅝"). FMCH X87.890.A,B.

34. TAPERSTICK. Silver.

Marks: London, sterling standard, 1735-36, maker's mark of James Gould (Grimwade no. 1317); marked under base, the socket with lion passant.

Height: 10.6 cm (4⅛"). FMCH X87.891.

35. CHOCOLATE POT. Silver.

Marks: Newcastle, sterling standard, 1734-35, maker's mark apparently FB; marked at lip, cover unmarked. The underneath of the base is engraved with initials RH.

Height: 25 cm (9¾"). FMCH X87.877.A,B.

36. (LEFT). **FOUR SALT CELLARS.** Silver.

Marks: London, Britannia standard, 1720-21, two with maker's mark of James Rood (Grimwade no. 2395), two with indistinct maker's mark; each marked under base. Each cellar is engraved with two sets of initials, H over TE and E over RS.

Width: 7.7 cm (3"). FMCH X87.843.A-D.

37. COFFEE POT. Silver and wood.

Marks: London, sterling standard, 1739-40, maker's mark of Peter Archambo (Grimwade no. 2128); hallmarked on rim, maker's mark under base, part marked on cover.

Height: 24.5 cm (9½"). FMCH X87.876.

38. PAIR OF SAUCEBOATS. Silver.

Marks: London, sterling standard, 1739-40, maker's mark of Paul de Lamerie (Grimwade no. 2204); marked under base, the marks on one sauceboat worn and illegible.

Heraldry: The crest is that of Anson for Admiral George Anson, Baron Anson of Soberton (1697-1762). *(See Cat. 1, page 23).*

Length: 18 cm (7"). FMCH X87.861.A,B.

39. WAITER. Silver.

Marks: London, Britannia standard, 1729-30, maker's mark of Paul de Lamerie (Grimwade no. 1892); marked on reverse.

Width: 14.2 cm (5½"). FMCH X87.860.

40. FOUR DISHES. Silver.

Marks: London, sterling standard, 1746-47, maker's mark of Paul de Lamerie (Grimwade no. 2204); each marked under rim.

Heraldry: The arms are those of Anson for Admiral George Anson, Baron Anson of Soberton (1697-1762). *(See Cat. 1, page 23).*

Diameter: 27.9 cm (10⅞").

FMCH X87.859.A-D.

41. DISH CROSS. Silver.

Marks: London, sterling standard, 1745-46, maker's mark of Paul de Lamerie (Grimwade no. 2204); marked under lamp, arms part marked, lamp cover unmarked.

Width: 29.3 cm (11½").

FMCH X87.867.A,B.

42. COFFEE POT. Silver and wood.

Marks: London, sterling standard, 1747-48, maker's mark of William Grundy (Grimwade no. 3147); marked under base and on cover.

Height: 28 cm (11"). FMCH X87.833.

See text, page 20.

43. QUAICH. Silver.

Marks: Edinburgh, sterling standard, 1761-62, maker's mark of William Dempster (Jackson p. 503); marked under base.

Heraldry: The arms on one handle are those of Pitcairn quartering Ramsey for Pitcairn of that Ilk, of Fifeshire; those on the other are for Campbell.

The quaich is a traditional Scottish drinking vessel and the engraved design on the sides represents the wooden hoops and staves from which such vessels were originally constructed.

Length: 28.5 cm (11⅛").

FMCH X87.1000.

44. BREAD BASKET. Silver.

Marks: London, sterling standard, 1750-51, maker's mark of Edward Aldridge (Grimwade no. 3534); marked on rim.

Heraldry: The arms are those of Shepard of Sussex and Mendlesham, Suffolk.

Length: 37cm (14½").

FMCH X87.816.

45. SALVER. Silver.

Marks: London, sterling standard, 1765-66, maker's mark of Thomas Hannam and John Crouch (Grimwade no. 2805); marked on the reverse.

Heraldry: The coat of arms on the dexter side is that of Otway, with Cave quartering Verney, Braye and Chamberlain (or Owen) in pretence, for Henry Otway of Castle Otway, County Tipperary (d. 1815), who in 1790 married Sarah, daughter of Sir Thomas Cave of Stanford Hall, Lutterworth, Leicestershire. That on the sinister side repeats the blazon shown in pretence on the dexter and is surmounted by a baron's coronet. In 1818, after the death of Henry Otway, his widow took the name of Otway-Cave and was declared in 1839 heir to the title Baroness Braye, which had been in abeyance since 1557. The engraving of this salver presumably dates from that time. The baroness died in 1862.

Diameter: 38.1 cm (14⅞").

FMCH X87.900.

46. TEA KETTLE, STAND AND LAMP.
Silver.

Marks: London, sterling standard, 1753-54, maker's mark of Richard Guerney and Thomas Cooke (Grimwade no. 2324); marked under base and on lamp.

Height: 29.5 cm (11½").

FMCH X87.1022.

47. EPERGNE. Silver.

Marks: London, sterling standard, 1763-64, maker's mark of Daniel Smith and Robert Sharp (Grimwade no. 3523); marked on rim of stand and under base of central basket, the smaller baskets and dishes marked and the branches unmarked.

The origin of the term "epergne" is unknown, although it refers to a kind of table centerpiece whose evolution can be traced to late 17th-century French silver. The type represented by the Fowler epergne was fashionable from the 1760s to the 1780s and, consisting only of baskets and shallow dishes, was intended for dessert. The leading maker of epergnes during the 1760s was Thomas Pitts, who may well have supplied this one to Smith and Sharp for retail.

Width: 66 cm (25¾"). FMCH X87.805.A-R.

48. CANDLESTICKS. Silver. (Two of a set of four).

Marks: London, sterling standard, 1755-56, maker's mark of William Grundy (Grimwade no. 3147); marked under bases, sockets part marked.

Height: 23 cm (9"). FMCH X87.865.A-H.

49. PAIR OF CANDLESTICKS. Silver.

Marks: London, sterling standard, 1760-61, maker's mark of William Cafe (Grimwade no. 3077); each marked under base, the sockets with lion passant only and the nozzles unmarked.

Heraldry: The coat of arms is unidentified.

Height: 23.4 cm (9⅛"). FMCH X87.889.A-D.

50. FOUR SALT CELLARS. Silver.

Marks: Dublin, Hibernia, two dated 1763-64, but lacking maker's mark and two lacking date letter, but with maker's mark of Robert Calderwood (Jackson p. 612).

Width: 10 cm (4"). FMCH X87.930.A-D.

51. PAIR OF SAUCEBOATS. Silver.

Marks: London, sterling standard, 1764-65, maker's mark of Daniel Smith and Robert Sharp (Grimwade no. 3523); marked under bases.

Each sauceboat is engraved with a later unidentified crest.

Length: 21 cm (8¼"). FMCH X87.885.A,B.

52. TWO PAIRS OF BEAKERS. Silver.

Marks: Chester, 1765-66 and 1767-68, maker's mark of Richard Richardson (Jackson p. 390); marked under base of each.

One pair is engraved under the bases with initials MD and the other with an unidentified crest.

Height: 16.8 cm (6½"), assembled. FMCH X87.868.A,B.

9.0 cm (3½"), 8.5 cm (3¼"). FMCH X87.869.A,B.

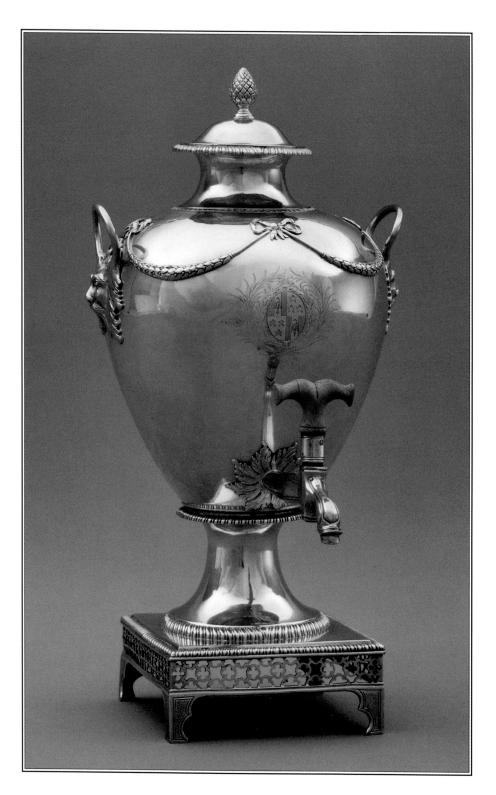

53. HOT WATER URN. Silver.

Marks: London, sterling standard, 1769-70, maker's mark of John Parker and Edward Wakelin (Grimwade no. 1602); marked on rim of detachable foot, inside body and part marked on rim of cover. The somewhat unusual construction of this urn incorporates a domed section at the base of the body, the interior of which is revealed by removing the foot and into which a pre-heated iron slug could be placed to keep the water hot. The engraved cartouche is contemporary and encloses a modern coat of arms.

Height: 39cm (15¼").

FMCH X87.1023.A-C.

54. TWO CUPS. Silver.

Marks: Dublin, one 1770-71, maker's mark of Charles Townsend (Jackson p. 612), the other 1772-73, maker's mark of Matthew West (Jackson p. 613); each marked on lip.

Height: 13.7cm (5⅜"). FMCH x87.866. 13.9cm (5½"). FMCH x87.927.

55. DISH RING. Silver.

Marks: Dublin, Hibernia, 1772-73, maker's mark of John Lloyd (Jackson p. 612); marked on lower rim.

Diameter: 20cm (7¾"). FMCH x87.933.

56. COVERED DISH. Silver. (One of a pair).

Marks: London, sterling standard, 1772-73, maker's mark of John Parker and Edward Wakelin (Grimwade no. 1602); each marked under dish and on rim of cover.

Heraldry: The crest is that of Fitzgerald for James, 20th Earl of Kildare (1722-73), who in 1766 was created Duke of Leinster.

These dishes are identical to and were presumably made to supplement those in the Leinster service of 1745-47, by George Wickes (see Cat. 31).

Width: 39.8cm (15½"). FMCH X87.884.A-D.

57. ARGYLL. Silver, wood and ivory.

Marks: London, sterling standard, 1772-73, maker's mark IC, possibly for John Carter II (Grimwade no. 1214); marked under base, part marked on cover and flap to smaller spout.

Heraldry: The crest is unidentified.

This is a double-skinned vessel for gravy, in which the cavity between the outer and inner wall is filled with hot water, thereby keeping the contents warm. The name refers to the Dukes of Argyll, one of whom is traditionally credited with inventing the device in the 18th century.

Length: 14.5cm (5⅝"). FMCH X87.871.A,B.

58. TWELVE DINNER PLATES. Silver.

Marks: London, sterling standard, 1778-79, seven with maker's mark of Robert Makepiece I and Richard Carter (Grimwade no. 2375), five with maker's mark of Richard Carter, Daniel Smith and Robert Sharp (Grimwade no. 2293); each marked under the rim.

Heraldry: The arms are those of Beresford quartering de la Poer, for Lord John George de la Poer Beresford (1773-1862), who was appointed primate of all Ireland in 1822. The second coat of arms is that of the See of Raphoe, impaling Beresford. Beresford was appointed Bishop of Cork and Ross in 1805 and translated to the See of Raphoe in 1807, where he remained until being appointed Bishop of Clogher in 1819. The engraving of these plates, therefore, dates from between 1807 and 1819.

Diameter: 24.6cm (9⅝"). FMCH X87.897.A-L.

59. TWO-HANDLED CREAM JUG. Silver.

Marks: London, sterling standard, 1782-83, maker's mark of John Scofield (Grimwade no. 1670); marked under base.

Height: 9cm (3½"). FMCH X87.880.

60. SAUCE TUREEN. Silver.
(One of a pair).

Marks: London, sterling standard, 1776-77, maker's mark of John Carter II (Grimwade no. 1214); each marked under base and on cover.

Each tureen is engraved with a contemporary cartouche, containing a later crest.

Width: 23.5 cm (9¼").

FMCH X87.872.A-D.

61. PAIR OF COCONUT GOBLETS.
Silver-gilt and coconut shell.

Marks: London, sterling standard, 1798-99, maker's mark of Hannah Northcote (Grimwade no. 1938); each marked on rim of foot and part marked inside gilt lining of bowl.

Heraldry: The crest and motto is that of Cathcart, possibly for William, 10th Baron Cathcart (1755-1843), who succeeded his father in 1776 and was advanced to the title Earl Cathcart in 1814.

Height: 19 cm (7½").

FMCH X87.969.A,B.

62. TRAY. Silver.

Marks: Dublin, Hibernia, 1788-89, maker's mark RB (probably for Robert Breading but unrecorded by Jackson); marked on reverse.

Heraldry: The arms are unidentified.

Width: 60.4 cm (23½"). FMCH X87.931.

63. (RIGHT). **DISH CROSS.** Silver.

Marks: London, sterling standard, 1793-94, maker's mark of Paul Storr (Grimwade no. 2234); marked on base of lamp, part marked on frame, the detachable arms unmarked.

Width: 30 cm (11¾").

FMCH X87.870.A-D.

64. (LEFT). **HOT WATER URN.** Silver.

Marks: Edinburgh, sterling standard, 1791-92, maker's mark of W. and P. Cunningham.

Heraldry: The crest and motto are those of Anderson.

Height: 59.7 cm (23¼").

FMCH X87.979.A-D.

65. TANKARD. Silver.

Marks: London, sterling standard, 1788-89, maker's mark of Charles Hougham (Grimwade no. 328), apparently over-striking another; marked on lip and part marked on cover. The tankard is engraved "WDS Feb. 29, 1908."

Height: 19.5 cm (7⅝"). FMCH X87.797.

66. CORKSCREW. Silver.

Marks: None. Probably made in England, late 18th century.

The corkscrew is engraved with initials IL.

Length: 11.5 cm (4½").

FMCH X87.962.

67. (LEFT). TWO PAIRS OF CANDLESTICKS. Silver.

Marks: London, sterling standard, 1796-97, maker's mark of John Scofield (Grimwade no. 1670); each marked on the rim of the foot, part marked on the nozzles.

Although made in the same year by the same maker and engraved with the same crest, these candlesticks are in fact two distinct pairs and have minor variations to the mouldings around the upper parts of the sticks.

Height: 32.8 cm (12¾").

FMCH X87.864.A-D. AND 883.A-D.

68. SAUCE TUREEN. Silver.

Marks: London, sterling standard, 1800-1, maker's mark of Paul Storr (Grimwade no. 2234); marked on rim of foot, part marked on cover and handle.

Width: 28.5 cm (11⅛").

FMCH X87.850.A,B. *See text, page 21.*

69. (LEFT). PAIR OF WINE COOLERS. Silver.

Marks: London, sterling standard, 1792-93, maker's mark of Edward Fennell (Grimwade no. 579); marked under base, on rim of liner and part marked on rim of collar.

Heraldry: The crest is unidentified.

Diameter: 20 cm (7¼").

FMCH X87.792.A-F.

70. ENTREE DISH AND COVER. Silver.

Marks: London, sterling standard, 1799-1800, maker's mark of Paul Storr (Grimwade no. 2234); marked on outside of dish, part marked inside cover and on handle.

Heraldry: The arms are unidentified.

Width: 24.2 cm (9"). FMCH X87.848.A,B.

Literature: Clayton 1985, pl. 260.

71. EGG CUP STAND. Silver.

Marks: Birmingham, sterling standard, 1800-1, maker's mark of Matthew Boulton (Jackson p. 408); marked on frame, the cups and casters each marked on foot, the caster covers part marked.

Width: 21.5 cm (8⅜").

FMCH X87.1021.A-K.

72. CRUET FRAME. Silver and glass.

Marks: London, sterling standard, 1800-1, maker's mark of Paul Storr (Grimwade no. 2234); marked under base; part marked on frame and bottle mounts.

Width: 40 cm (15⅝").

FMCH X87.854.A-L.

73. ENTREE DISH AND COVER.
Silver. (One of a set of four).

Marks: London, sterling standard, 1801-2, maker's mark of Henry Chawner and Jonathan Emes (Grimwade no. 977); each marked on dish and cover, part marked on detachable coronet.

Heraldry: The engraving of the charges on the coat of arms is too worn to be clearly legible and the arms are consequently unidentified. They are, however, surmounted by a baron's coronet and are contained within a lozenge-shaped shield indicating a woman.

Width: 30.7 cm (12").

FMCH X87.896.A-L.

74. DISH. Silver. (One of a pair).

Marks: London, sterling standard, 1805-6, maker's mark of Paul Storr (Grimwade no. 2234); each marked on the outside.

Heraldry: The arms are those of Foley for Thomas, third Baron Foley (1780-1833) who in 1806 married Lady Cecilia Olivia Geraldine Fitzgerald, fifth daughter of William Robert, second Duke of Leinster.

Width: 28.8 cm (11¼").

FMCH X87.846.A,B.

75. PAIR OF WINE COOLERS. Silver.

Marks: London, sterling standard, 1806-7, maker's mark of John Parker II (Grimwade no. 3670); each marked on foot rim, part marked on liners and collars.

Heraldry: The arms are possibly those of Curtis of Clinton, Warwickshire, impaling Blathwaite or Brainthwaite.

Height: 23.5 cm (9¼").

FMCH X87.791.A-F.

76. VEGETABLE DISH AND COVER.

Silver. (One of a pair).

Marks: London, sterling standard, 1809-10, maker's mark of Paul Storr (Grimwade no. 2234); each marked on side of dish, part marked on cover and handle.

Heraldry: The crest and motto are unidentified.

Width: 27 cm (10½") FMCH X87.853.A-D.

77. TOAST RACK. Silver.

Marks: London, sterling standard, 1809-10, maker's mark of Paul Storr (Grimwade no. 2234); marked under base, part marked on detachable bars.

Width: 24 cm (9⅜"). FMCH X87.849.

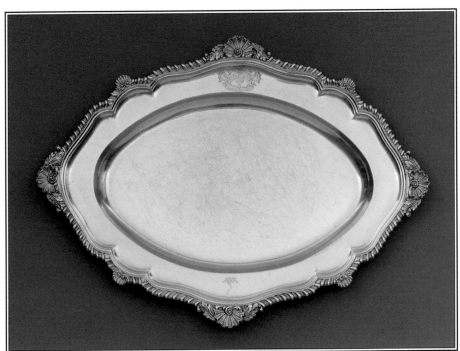

78. MEAT DISH. Silver.

Marks: London, sterling standard, 1810-11, maker's mark of Thomas Robins (Grimwade no. 2915); marked under rim.

Heraldry: The arms are those of Duncombe with Field in pretence.

Width: 48.2 cm (18⅝"). FMCH X87.939.

79. GOBLET. Silver-gilt.

Marks: London, sterling standard, 1811-12, maker's mark
of Rebecca Emes and Edward Barnard (Grimwade no. 2309);
marked on rim of foot.

Height: 15.5 cm (6"). FMCH X87.1026.

80. (LEFT). **SOUP TUREEN AND STAND.** Silver.

Marks: London, sterling standard, 1804-5 (the stand 1810-11),
maker's mark of Paul Storr (Grimwade no. 2234); marked on rim
of tureen, under base of stand and part marked on rim of cover
and handle.

Heraldry: The arms are those of Eden, probably quartering
Johnson, and are presumably for Sir Robert Johnson-Eden,
5th baronet (1774-1844), who assumed the arms and surname of
Johnson by royal license on February 15, 1811, and died unmarried.
The engraving is thus of slightly later date than the tureen.

Width: 54.5 cm (21¼"). FMCH X87.815.A-C.

81. COFFEE POT. Silver and ivory.

Marks: London, sterling standard,
1812-13, maker's mark of Paul Storr (Grimwade no. 2234);
marked under base, part marked on cover.

Heraldry: The arms are later and are those of Robertson of Kindeace,
Rosshire, Scotland.

Height: 21.1 cm (8¼"). FMCH X87.851.

See text, page 21.

82. BACON DISH. Silver and wood.

Marks: Sterling standard, 1822-23 (the inner tray 1824-25), maker's mark of Paul Storr (Grimwade no. 2234); marked under base, part marked on cover and on tray.

Heraldry: The arms are those of Pelham Clinton for Henry, fourth Duke of Newcastle (1785-1851). The duke married in 1807 Georgina Elizabeth, daughter of Edward Miller Mundy Esq., and was steward and keeper of Sherwood Forest. The inner tray is engraved with the star and badge of the Order of the Garter.

Width: 27 cm (9¾"). FMCH X87.852.A-C.

83. EWER AND DISH. Silver, parcel-gilt.

Marks: London, sterling standard, 1863-64, maker's mark of Stephen Smith and William Nicholson (Culme no. 13596); marked on lip of ewer and near center of dish.

Height: 37 cm (14½").

FMCH X87.1024.A,B.

84. MEAT DISH. Silver.

Marks: London, sterling standard, 1817-18, maker's mark of Joseph Cradock and William K. Reid (Grimwade no. 1236); marked under rim.

Heraldry: The arms on the dexter side are unidentified, impaling Eales.

Width: 61.9 cm (24⅛"). FMCH X87.940.

85. (ABOVE). **TWELVE DINNER PLATES.** Silver.

Marks: London, sterling standard, 1813-14, maker's mark of Paul Storr (Grimwade no. 2234); each marked under rim.

Heraldry: The crest is unidentified, although the coronet is that of a baron.

Diameter: 25.5cm (10"). FMCH X87.858.

86. (LEFT). **SALVER.** Silver.

Marks: London, sterling standard, 1829-30, maker's mark of Barnard and Co. (Grimwade no. 575); marked under rim.

Heraldry: The arms are those of Foster impaling Freeman.

Diameter: 63cm (24½"). FMCH X87.1025.

87. INKSTAND. Silver and glass.

Marks: London, sterling standard, 1848-49, maker's mark of John and Joseph Angell (Grimwade no. 1772); marked near top of dome, the cover part marked.

Heraldry: The arms are those of Campbell impaling another.

Diameter: 18.0cm (7"). FMCH X87.942.

88. TWELVE COVERED GOBLETS. Silver-gilt. Probably c.1830.

Marks: None.

Heraldry: The arms are those of Augustus Frederick, Duke of Sussex (1773-1843), third son of George III, and each cup is engraved with "HRH Duke of Sussex" and a royal ducal crown. Four of the cups are additionally engraved with the arms of Francis, first Earl Brooke and first Earl of Warwick (1719-1773) and with the inscription "The Gift of HRH Duke of Sussex To The EARL of WARWICK 1760."

Height: 34cm (13¼"). FMCH X87.1028.

See text, page 22, for a full discussion of these problematic cups, including the chronological discrepancy.

89. PAIR OF RHYTONS.
Silver, parcel-gilt.

Marks: London, sterling standard, 1886-87, maker's mark of George Fox (Culme no. 5745); marked at lip.

These are replicas of a type of ancient Greek vessel. Made in the form of a horn and generally terminating in an animal's head, they are found in both pottery and silver from the fifth century B.C.

Height: 13.6 cm (5¼"). FMCH X87.1017.

90. TANKARD. Silver.

Marks: London, sterling standard, 1815-16, maker's mark of William Elliot (Grimwade no. 3107); marked on lip, part marked on cover.

Height: 19.5 cm (7⅝"). FMCH X87.803.

See text, page 22.

CONTINENTAL EUROPEAN SILVER

WESTERN EUROPEAN SILVER

The continental European silver in the Fowler collection consists mainly of German and Russian pieces. The concentration on vessels of German origin is more or less forced on the collector who wishes to obtain pieces dating from the seventeenth century or earlier. The high rate of survival of German silver vessels seems at first surprising; German treasuries and silver collections were devastated during the Thirty Years War and suffered repeated spoliation during the dynastic wars of the eighteenth century, during the Napoleonic wars, and again in the World Wars of the twentieth century. The reasons for its survival are various: the large number of small principalities each with their court and ruling prince; the fact that in the cities both the city councils and the guilds accumulated vessels of pre-

Detail of shoemakers' guild cup. FMCH X87.973.
(See Cat. 91, page 85).

cious metal; and, finally, the huge production of the south German goldsmiths of Nuremberg and Augsburg, who exported silver all over Europe. The fact that so much has survived can, therefore, be explained by the circumstance that so much was in existence to begin with. Much remained in the possession of the original owners until the nineteenth century, and when, as a result of political and economic changes, it was dispersed, instead of being melted down into bullion as would have happened in previous centuries, it was

bought up by collectors and lovingly preserved.

The earliest continental pieces in the collection are guild cups (Cat. 91 and 92). It was the practice of the German guilds to commission cups whose design reflected, as far as was practicable, the nature of the craft they exercised. These two were evidently made for shoemakers' guilds. The shoemakers were not among the wealthier guilds and this fact may well have played some part in the design of the cups, made almost entirely of leather with no more than a silver collar around the top. One of the two is engraved with the arms of the city of Memmingen in Swabia, showing that it must have belonged to the shoemakers' guild of that small town.

The other cup is engraved with a lion hunt and an amorous couple about to be disturbed by a bear, which gives no clue as to its origin. The bell attached to the end mount of the shoe contributed to the jollity of guild assemblies, or was perhaps shaken to indicate that the cup was empty. The occasions that might lead to such a cup being acquired by the guild were various; it might be presented by a warden of the guild on completion of his year in office, by a journeyman on admission as master of his craft or, perhaps, in lieu of a fine, by a guild member who had committed some minor offense against the guild regulations. This was not an infrequent occurrence as the guild controlled every aspect of the member's life, including attendance at church services, business probity, and sexual morality.

Judging by the number of surviving vessels of this type, drinking cups wrought in the form of human figures or animals were particularly fashionable during the latter decades of the sixteenth and most of the seventeenth century. The Fowler collection has a representative series, all of German origin. The most original of these is the wild boar cup (Cat. 95). This is the work of the Augsburg goldsmith Paul Kleebühler. The head, legs, and tail are of gilt silver while the body, fashioned from a coconut, is carved to resemble the boar's pelt. Coconut cups were popular at this period and many examples have survived; the nut did not lend itself easily to human or animal form, though a few owl cups are known. No other example of a wild boar cup fashioned from a coconut appears to be recorded.

The collection also includes a bull, two horses, and a lion. Of these the most finely modeled is undoubtedly the rampant bull

Detail from base of cup in the form of a horse. FMCH X87.971. *(See Cat. 98, page 88).*

(Cat. 94) made by the Lüneburg master Heinrich Frantz Gorich. According to a tradition communicated to its former owner, J. Pierpont Morgan, this cup originally belonged to the Butchers' Guild of the Swiss city of Basel. As was usually the case with such cups wrought in the form of human figures or animals, the head formed a cover and could be removed in order for the cup to be used as a drinking vessel. It would not be correct, however, to assume that such cups were often put to practical use: they were treated more as decorative objects and adorned the sideboard at guild functions. The works of the south German masters so outnumber those of the northern cities that the importance of the latter tends to be underestimated. Only the chance survival of the greater part of the Lüneburg city council treasure, now in the Schloss Charlottenburg Museum in Berlin, has established the abundant skill of the Lüneburg masters and the great size and splendor of their productions.

The lively horse (Cat. 98) bears the mark of the Augsburg master, Heinrich Mannlich, who was admitted a master goldsmith in the Czech town of Troppau in 1649 but soon sought a more promising future in Augsburg, where he set up in 1651. The base, the lowest part of which was reshaped at a later date, is embossed with grasses and leaves and further embellished with minute cast figures of newts and lizards in continuation of the fashion which was first introduced by Wenzel Jamnitzer of Nuremberg about a century earlier. Such conservatism is not by any means unusual in German seventeenth-century goldsmiths' work, but a more typical baroque base can be seen on another lion cup, this time by a Hamburg goldsmith (Cat. 96). In this case the rampant lion stands on a circular base boldly embossed with swirling baroque foliage of a type which was particularly favored by Dutch and northwestern goldsmiths. A small shield enameled with a coat of arms probably records the identity of the donor who originally presented it to the treasury of some north German guild. The production of such figures, which were wrought from sheet and not cast, was extremely complex for the goldsmith. The body was worked up from flat plate in several pieces, each being soldered up the seam. The legs and arms and tail were cast and attached separately and the point where the lion's right leg and haunch are joined is clearly visible. The part most difficult to make was the head, which was again hollow and had to be worked up from the flat plate, embossed and chased with the details of the hair, ears and eyes. The finest equestrian figures were made by Augsburg goldsmiths of the seventeenth century. Goldsmiths in other cities worked in the same manner – as in the case of the rearing horse (Cat. 97) by a Liegnitz master probably dating from the last years of the seventeenth century; but the provincial goldsmiths achieved a naive charm rather than

the sculptural distinction of the more prominent Augsburg masters.

Drinking cups modeled in the form of human figures were made in two different forms during the seventeenth century. In one case, the figure itself constituted the drinking vessel and the removable head served as a cover, like the animal figure cups described above. In the second type the figure was wrought separately from the drinking vessel, which was usually a beaker attached to the back of the figure. The most popular version was the so-called Büttenman or Büttenfrau, a man or woman in contemporary dress each bearing on his or her back a beaker formed like a basket for harvesting grapes. The beaker was lightly attached so that it could easily be removed for drinking. Of the two types the standing figures were the less convenient for drinking and were for the most part probably admired as examples of the goldsmiths' ingenuity. The Fowler collection includes a pair of "Bütten" figures – a man and a woman (Cat. 103). Apart from the heads, hands, and feet, these figures are entirely worked up from flat plate; this involved an immense amount of work, quite apart from the initial problem of procuring a model to copy. They bear the mark of a Danzig goldsmith and can be dated on the grounds of costume to the beginning of the seventeenth century. Danzig is not a wine-growing region, though the man holds a tall beaker in his hand. The woman, however, holds a fish, suggesting that she is meant to represent a fishwife, a suitable trade for Danzig.

The earliest of all the tankards in the collection is the work of an anonymous Vienna goldsmith who used the initials MS (Cat. 104). The rat-tail ornament attached to the back of the handle dates it to the beginning of the seventeenth century, but it has been enriched at a later date by the insertion in the drum and in the cover of a number of coins and medals on Habsburg Holy Roman Emperors, including those of Ferdinand I as King of Hungary, Dalmatia and Croatia (1541), of the Emperor Ferdinand II (1563), and of Maximilian II (1577). The goldsmith who altered the tankard, probably not so very long after it was made, showed great ingenuity in adapting the design to accept the circular forms of the coins and medals.

The Augsburg tankard (Cat. 107) illustrates once again the conservative tendency of the goldsmith. Although hardly earlier than 1710, the boldly embossed baroque foliage which adorns it recalls the pattern book designs of the middle years of the preceding century. During the eighteenth century, fashion in western Europe was usually dictated by Paris; whereas in central and eastern Europe the goldsmiths looked to Augsburg for new ideas, not infrequently because they had themselves been trained in Augsburg or had even emigrated from that city after completing their training there. The tall covered beaker (Cat. 109), bearing a Moscow mark and the date letter for 1738, well illustrates the influence of Augsburg far beyond the German frontiers.

Vast quantities of domestic plate were owned by the electors of Bavaria, much of which is still preserved in the

ABOVE, LEFT: Detail of "Büttenfrau" figure. FMCH X87.976.C. *(See Cat. 103, page 92).*
BELOW: Detail of tankard. FMCH X87.977. *(See Cat. 104, page 93).*

silver room of the Munich Residence. Among the few pieces to have left Munich is the Augsburg beaker (Cat. 112). It is dated 1799, the year in which the elector Maximilian Joseph II acceded to the throne. It was presumably part of the plate that was ordered for his coronation year.

The late Mr. Fowler anticipated long ago the present interest in nineteenth-century decorative art. Among the wealth of examples of this period the monumental teapot (Cat. 99) is worthy of particular attention. As the nineteenth century progressed and industrial techniques were developed, individually designed and executed pieces were less frequently produced. In this Italian vessel we find the signatures of two separate masters: of Bianchi the designer and Landi the goldsmith. While nothing is known of the

former, the latter is recorded as working in Lucca and it is presumably from this town that the teapot originates. Of dignified form, it corresponds to the type of vessel that was being produced by Storr and Mortimer in the late 1830s, but the ornament, instead of being cast, as on a Storr piece, is entirely chased.

RUSSIAN SILVER

The most comprehensive body of nineteenth-century silver in the collection is of Russian origin. Goldsmiths had flourished in Moscow since at least the Middle Ages and a system of hallmarking had been introduced in 1613. Under conditions of exceptional patronage, such as existed in the Kremlin during the second half of the seventeenth century, objects of outstanding beauty and sophistication were produced. But for ordinary domestic plate, goldsmiths and

their customers showed a marked adherence to traditional vessel types; thus forms such as the *kovsch*, *bratina* and *charka* continued with very little development throughout the seventeenth and eighteenth centuries. For covered cups and other decorative plate, goldsmiths were strongly influenced by German models, although often with a considerable interval between their appearance in Germany and their adoption in Russia. The covered cup (Cat. 110) was made in Moscow in 1748 and although its decoration betrays its period, its form and the treatment of the stem and finial are all derived from a type popular in Nuremberg during the early seventeenth century. Similarly, the Moscow dish of 1710 (Cat. 108) is chased with foliage and abstract relief decoration reminiscent of western Europe in the middle of the previous century.

The Russian nineteenth-century silver in the collection falls mainly into two groups, decorated either with *niello* or polychrome enamel. Niello is an amalgam composed of copper, silver, lead, and sulphur and has been known from ancient times. Once formed, the amalgam is ground to a fine powder, applied in a paste to the surface of the object and fired in a kiln. This causes the powder to melt and fuse to the

ABOVE: Detail of tankard. FMCH X87.959. *(See Cat. 107, page 94).*
LEFT: Detail of dish. FMCH X87.953. *(See Cat. 108, page 94).*

ABOVE: Detail of tea service. FMCH x87.831. *(See Cat. 122, page 102).*
BELOW, RIGHT: Detail of kovsch. FMCH x87.994. *(See Cat. 100, page 90).*

tury these traditional techniques were revived and developed with enormous success by jeweler-retailers such as Ovchinnikov and Fabergé. Enamel is a form of polychrome decoration achieved by grinding vitreous sands mixed with metallic oxides into a fine powder and fusing it to the surface under heat. Like niello, it is of great antiquity, but was perfected in the Middle Ages when a number of quite distinct techniques were developed. Two broad categories, known respectively as *champlevé* and *cloisonné,* were used in Europe. The first, meaning literally "raised field," includes several techniques all of which involved laying enamel into a recessed area of the surface so that when finished the enamel is flush with the surrounding metal. In the later Middle Ages, *basse-taille* represented a further refinement of the technique by the introduction of translucent enamel which allowed the underlying metal to reflect the light to varying degrees, depending on the depth of the enamel. In nineteenth-century Russia the most common type of enamel was cloisonné, a technique originally developed by Byzantine goldsmiths in which the surface was divided into separate compartments by small fillets of gold, each of

surface. It is then allowed to cool and is polished. The technique gradually disappeared from the western goldsmith's repertoire after the Middle Ages and although it was never completely abandoned in Russia, it has been suggested that its revival in the late seventeenth century was largely due to the influx of refugee jewelers from Constantinople into Moscow during the 1660s.

The earliest use of niello was to flood engraved decoration, thereby heightening the contrast and increasing the definition of the design. In the seventeenth century it was also painted onto the surface in tightly scrolling floral patterns as a ground for other gilded and engraved decoration. By this means an extraordinarily rich and varied range of surface textures could be achieved. The most dramatic use of niello in the Fowler collection is on the Moscow tea service of 1895 (Cat. 122), in which the niello foliage is raised in relief above the plain gilded ground. In the late nineteenth century many tea services and smaller objects such as cigarette cases were made with depictions of well-known buildings or monuments, often enhanced with niello. That at least some of these were made specifically for export is clear from the inscription on the 1895 tankard (Cat. 114), "Made for Tiffany & Co," the New York retailers.

Enameled decoration had also long been part of the Russian goldsmith's repertoire and in the nineteenth cen-

which was individually soldered to the back plate before the enameling was carried out. The grandest piece in this technique in the Fowler collection is the large kovsch (Cat. 100) in which the divisions have been formed by twisted threads and the opaque enamel has been heightened by painted enamel details.

Translucent enamel was also popular among nineteenth-century Russian goldsmiths, especially in a type known as *plique-à-jour*. In this technique, used for the cigarette case (Cat. 93), a filigree framework is entirely filled with trans-lucent enamel to produce an effect resembling miniature stained glass.

While snuff boxes and other small-scale works by Fabergé were often inspired by French eighteenth-century gold-smiths' work, much of the decorative plate from his and other workshops reflected an increasing interest in Russia's cultural roots and looked to traditional forms and to Eastern rather than Western techniques and styles. But a similar interest in historicism was evident throughout Europe in the second half of the nineteenth century. Many objects made in medieval or Renaissance taste were produced with flagrantly dishonest motives, but many also were made simply to satisfy a demand for objects in an antique taste. Three such objects in the Fowler collection are the two cups (Cat. 125 and 126) and the French altar cruet set (Cat. 120). The cups are both derived from well known early sixteenth-century drawings and bear the mark of Berthold Müller, a major importer in England of German decorative silver-ware during the late nineteenth and early twentieth centu-ries. The cruet set likewise bears the proper French marks for its time and has been made with no intention to deceive. But it clearly reflects the interest in French decorative arts of the Renaissance that was developing during the latter part of the century, especially in the painted grisaille enamel plaques that are inspired by the sixteenth-century enamels for which Limoges was famous.

Reverse of Russian cigarette case. *(See opposite, Cat. 93).*

91. (ABOVE, LEFT). **SHOEMAKERS' GUILD CUP.**
Silver and leather. Germany, c. 1500.

Marks: None.

Both the sole and the heel have a small inset pane of glass, beneath which are a gaming die and a small piece of inscribed parchment.

Length: 17 cm (6⅝"). FMCH X87.973.

See text, page 79. Literature: Hayward 1976, p. 524, where it is given as third quarter, 16th century.

92. (ABOVE, RIGHT). **SHOEMAKERS' GUILD CUP.**
Silver-gilt and leather. Germany, early 16th century.

Marks: None.

Heraldry: The arms are those of the city of Memmingen in Swabia.

Length: 18 cm (7"). FMCH X87.974.

See text, page 79.

93. CIGARETTE CASE. Silver-gilt and plique-à-jour enamel. Russia.

Marks: Moscow, 84 standard, 1891, maker's mark of Pavel Ovchinnikov; marked on rim.

Length: 9.1 cm (3⅜"). FMCH X87.999.

94. CUP IN THE FORM OF A BULL. Silver-gilt. Germany, c. 1700.

Marks: Lüneburg, maker's mark of Heinrich Frantz Gorich (Scheffler no. 2315); marked on rim of detachable head.

Height: 25.5 cm (10"). FMCH X87.972.A,B.

95. CUP IN THE FORM OF A SOW. Silver-gilt and coconut shell. Germany, c. 1600.

Marks: Augsburg, maker's mark of Paul Kleebühler (Seling no. 944); marked on rim of detachable head.

Length: 18 cm (7"). FMCH X87.978.A,B.

See text, page 80.

**96. CUP IN THE FORM
OF A RAMPANT LION.** Silver-gilt.
Germany, c. 1650.

Marks: Hamburg, maker's mark of
Jurgen Richels (Schliemann no. 245);
marked on base.

Heraldry: The enameled coat of arms on
the base is that of Kefer von Ettenkofen
of Bavaria.

The lion was originally made to support
a large heraldic shield between its paws;
a very similar lion, also missing its shield,
is in the Kremlin Museum in Moscow
(see Schliemann pl. 40).

Height: 41 cm (16"). FMCH X87.982.A,B.

See text, page 80.

97. CUP IN THE FORM OF A REARING HORSE. Silver-gilt. Germany, c. 1700.

Marks: Liegnitz, maker's mark TW in a lobed punch (unrecorded by Rosenberg); marked on lip, base with maker's mark.

Height: 29 cm (11¼"). FMCH X87.981.A,B.

See text, page 80.

98. CUP IN THE FORM OF A HORSE. Silver-gilt. Germany, c. 1670.

Marks: Augsburg, maker's mark of Heinrich Mannlich (Seling no. 1613); marked on rim of base.

Height: 20.1 cm (7¾"). FMCH X87.971.A,B.

See text, page 80.

99. TEAPOT. Silver-gilt. Italy, c. 1840.

Marks: LP in a triangle, G in a lozenge; marked on foot.
Also signed "BIANCHI INV. LANDI ESEG."

The maker, Carlo Landi, is recorded as a goldsmith and seal
engraver. A native of Vincenzo, he was working in Lucca between
1833 and 1846.

Height: 29.9cm (11⅝"). FMCH X87.970.

See text, page 82.

100. **KOVSCH.** Silver-gilt and cloisonné enamel. Russia, c. 1900.

Marks: 84 standard, maker's mark E P; marked under base
and on foot rim.

Length: 28.3 cm (11"). FMCH X87.994.

101. PAIR OF TANKARDS AND A FLAGON. Silver-gilt. Russia.

Marks: Moscow, 84 standard, 1862, maker's mark of Ivan Semenovich Gubkin; marked under bases, other parts part marked. Each is engraved "Presented to Mᵉ Edward G. Sykes, by his English Friends residing in and near to Moscow - July 8th. 1862." and with the crest of Sykes. The tankards are also engraved with views of the Kremlin and on the cover with a rooster.

Height of tankards: 15.4cm (6"). FMCH X87.990.A,B.

Height of flagon: 27.5cm (10¾"). FMCH X87.991.

102. **LADLE.** Silver.
Roman Empire, probably first
or second century AD.

Marks: None.
Length: 27.5cm (10¾").
FMCH X87.966.

103. **PAIR OF FIGURES**
(Büttenman, Büttenfrau).
Silver, parcel-gilt.
Germany, early 17th century.

Marks: Danzig, maker's mark GF
(unrecorded by Rosenberg); marked
under detachable barrels. The base of
each figure is struck with a further
unidentified mark.

Height: 17.0cm (6⅝"). (Büttenman).
FMCH X87.976.A,B.

16.8cm (6½"). (Büttenfrau).
FMCH X87.976.C,D.

See text, page 81.

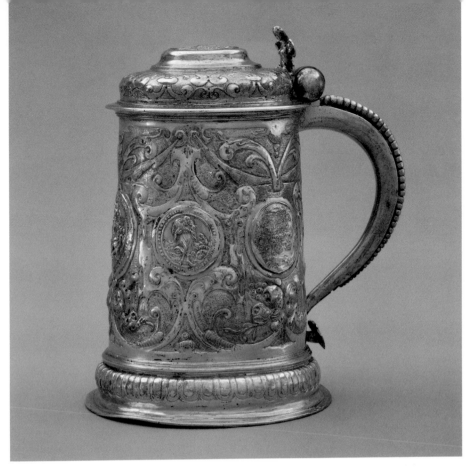

104. TANKARD. Silver-gilt. Austria, c. 1630.

Marks: Vienna, maker's mark MS; marked on foot.

Height: 18 cm (7").

FMCH X87.977.

See text, page 81.

105. TANKARD. Silver, parcel-gilt. Germany, c. 1660.

Marks: Augsburg, maker's mark of Daniel Schwestermüller (Seling no. 1721); marked on cover and foot.

Height: 15.8 cm (6¼").

FMCH X87.941.

106. (ABOVE, LEFT). **BEAKER.** Silver, parcel-gilt.
Germany, c. 1660.

Marks: Augsburg, maker's mark of Philip Jakob IV Drentwett
(Seling no. 2094); marked under base.

Height: 13.5cm (5¼"). FMCH x87.961.

107. (ABOVE, RIGHT). **TANKARD.** Silver, parcel-gilt.
Germany, c. 1700.

Marks: Augsburg, maker's mark of Erhard Warnberger
(Seling no. 1892a); marked on lip, cover and under base.

Height: 18.5cm (7¼"). FMCH x87.959.

See text, page 81.

108. DISH. Silver.
Russia.

Marks: Moscow date mark for 1710 (town mark lacking),
maker's mark indistinct.

Diameter: 24.4cm (9½"). FMCH x87.953. *See text, page 82.*

109. (ABOVE). **COVERED BEAKER.** Silver, parcel-gilt.
Russia.

Marks: Moscow, 1738, maker's mark MFK in monogram
(Goldberg no. 903); marked under base and on cover.

Height: 24.5cm (9½"). FMCH X87.997.A,B. *See text, page 81.*

110. (RIGHT). **CUP AND COVER.** Silver-gilt.
Russia.

Marks: Moscow, 1748, maker's mark GG; marked on foot,
lip, cover, and stem.

Height: 41cm (16"). FMCH X87.837.A,B.

III. (LEFT). **SEAL BOX.** Silver-gilt. Germany.

Marks: Dresden, date letter G, probably for 1756, maker's mark Gebr S, probably for Gebruder Schrodel (cf. Rosenberg no. 1815); marked on rim of lower part.

Heraldry: The arms are those of Friedrich Christian of Saxony (1722-63), who in 1747 married Maria Antonia Walurga, second daughter of Karl VII Albrecht, Holy Roman Emperor and Elector of Bavaria. He succeeded his father in 1763, two months before his own death.

Diameter: 13.5cm (5¼").

FMCH X87.839.A,B.

112. (FAR LEFT). **COVERED BEAKER.**

Silver, parcel-gilt.

Germany.

Marks: Augsburg, 1799, maker's mark of Caspar Xavier Stippeldey (Seling no. 2505); marked under base, the cover unmarked.

Heraldry: The arms are almost certainly those of Maximilian I, King of Bavaria (1756-1825), who succeeded his brother Karl as Duke of Zweibrucken in 1795, and Elector Karl Theodor as Elector of Bavaria and Elector Palatine in 1799. He married Maria Wilhelmine Auguste, youngest daughter of Prince Georg Wilhelm of Hessen-Darmstadt, in 1785. In 1805, when Bavaria became a kingdom, he assumed the title of King of Bavaria. The arms were altered in that same year.

Height: 17 cm (6⅝"). FMCH X87.958.A,B.

See text, page 82.

113. (LEFT). **BEAKER.**

Silver and cloisonné enamel.

Russia.

Marks: Moscow, 84 standard, 1883, maker's mark of Pavel Ovchinnikov; marked under base.

Height: 16.1 cm (6¼"). FMCH X87.986.

114. (RIGHT, ABOVE). **TANKARD.**

Silver and niello.

Russia.

Marks: Moscow, 84 standard, 1895, maker's mark AIK; marked under base. In addition to the marks, the tankard is also stamped under the base "Made for Tiffany & Co," the New York retailers.

Height: 19 cm (7½"). FMCH X87.987.

115. (RIGHT). **SAUCEPAN.**

Silver and wood.

France.

Marks: Paris, *charge*, 1780-81, *décharge*, maker's mark of Claude-Isaac Bourgoin (Beuque no. 312); marked under base and on cover.

Width: 20.3 cm (8"). FMCH X87.944.A,B.

116. OIL AND VINEGAR FRAME. Silver.
France.

Marks: Paris, 1st standard (95%), 1819-38, maker's mark lacking.

Height: 40 cm (15⅝"). FMCH X87.965.A-I.

117. MASSIVE TANKARD. Silver-gilt.

Russia, 1874.

Marks: None.

Heraldry: The arms are those of HRH Prince Alfred Ernest, Duke of Edinburgh, who was the second son of Queen Victoria. He was born on August 6, 1844, and died July 30, 1900. The inscription under the base may be translated: "His Imperial Majesty the Emperor Alexander Nikolaevich graciously consented to have this vessel made in honor of the visit of His Royal Highness Prince Alfred Ernest Albert, Duke of Edinburgh, to St. Petersburg, 1874." This visit was presumably the one made on the occasion of the prince's marriage to Grand Duchess Maria Alexandrovna, daughter of Alexander II, which took place on January 23 of that year. The inscription on the lower terminal of the handle translates "Court manufacturer Sazikov."

Height: 33.5cm (13"). FMCH X87.995.

118. FLAGON. Silver, parcel-gilt. Russia.

Marks: Moscow, 84 standard, 1855, maker's mark of Ivan Semenovich Gubkin; marked under base, other parts part marked.

Height: 25 cm (9¾"). FMCH X87.998.

119. VESSEL.
Silver, glazed stoneware and enamel. Russia, c. 1900.

Marks: 88 standard, maker's mark of Karl Fabergé; marked on mount.

Width: 13 cm (5"). FMCH X87.993.

120. ALTAR CRUET SET.
Silver-gilt and enamel.
France, late 19th century.

Marks: 1st standard (95%), maker's mark PD, mitre between; marked under stand and on cruet bottle and covers. The stand is inscribed in enamel "Sanguis Christi inebria me Aqua Lateris Christi Lava me." The enameled scenes on the stand show four scenes from the story of Isaac; those on the bottles illustrate various other Old and New Testament stories.

Width: 29.8 cm (11⅝"). FMCH X87.1015.A-D.

121. KOVSCH. Silver, cloisonné enamel.
Russia, c. 1900.

Marks: 88 standard, maker's mark E P
Length: 12.8 cm (5"). FMCH X87.985.

122. (LEFT). **TEA SERVICE.**
Silver-gilt and niello.
Russia.

Marks: Moscow, 84 standard, 1895, maker's mark of Maria Semenovna; marked under bases and part marked on covers.

Height: 13.0 cm (5"). FMCH X87.831.A-E.

123. (BELOW, FAR LEFT). **BEAKER.**
Silver-gilt and niello.
Russia.

Marks: Moscow, 84 standard, 1845, maker's mark ee; marked under base.

Height: 9.3 cm (3⅝"). FMCH X87.945.

124. (BELOW, LEFT). **TANKARD.**
Silver-gilt and cloisonné enamel.
Russia, c. 1900.

Marks: 84 standard, maker's mark T; marked under base.

Height: 11.5 cm (4½"). FMCH X87.989.

125. (RIGHT). **DOUBLE CUP.** Silver-gilt.
Germany.

Marks: Maker's mark of Berthold Müller, London import marks for 1907-8; each cup marked on lip.

The design of this cup is taken directly from a drawing of 1526 by Albrecht Dürer in the Albertina, Vienna (Hayward pl. 30).

Height: 38.0 cm (14¾). FMCH X87.975.A,B.

126. CUP AND COVER. Silver-gilt.
Germany.

Marks: Maker's mark of Berthold
Müller, Chester import marks for
1904-5; marked on lip and on cover.

Height: 44.0 cm (17⅛").

FMCH X87.951.A,B.

AMERICAN SILVER

The American silver in the Fowler collection is by far the smallest of the three groups, but nevertheless does represent the most characteristic eighteenth-century forms and the most famous makers of that century. During the colonial period American silversmiths and their patrons, for obvious reasons, were heavily influenced by contemporary styles in England. Many of the buyers, being first or second generation immigrants from England, naturally took their lead from London fashions; and many of the silversmiths had a similar background. Moreover, close regulation of trade in the colonies ensured a ready market in America for finished English goods, to the detriment of those from other countries. At the same time, however, the operation of certain other factors led to the evolution of a style and range of plate that was specifically American and distinct from English silver.

The most important patrons of English silversmiths had always been the aristocracy, and fashion had generally tended to filter down from that level to the lower end of the market. In America there was no aristocracy, and this circumstance was reflected in what might be termed a less courtly and more conservative aspect to the decorative arts. While furniture and silver of fine quality were produced in centers such as Philadelphia and Boston, these objects were seldom produced solely for display, but to be useful as well as beautiful. Similarly, the enormous sums of surplus capital that were needed to commission the ewers and basins, wine cisterns and great dinner services of early eighteenth-century England were not available in America, and the heirlooms passed through generations of American families tended to be the more practical domestic plate of a middle class society, such as tankards, caudle cups, and tea silver.

The majority of silversmiths in pre-revolutionary America worked in New York, Boston, and Philadelphia. There were many fewer in the southern colonies, probably on account of the fact that wealth there was based on land rather than trade, and craftsmen tended to enjoy a lower reputation there than in the urban north. The wealthy families of the

Detail of Joseph Richardson bowl. FMCH x87.912. *(See Cat. 130, page 108).*

south generally preferred to order their plate directly from London than to have it supplied locally, and were better able to afford to do so. This is clearly indicated by the records of the annual exports of finished plate to the colonies between 1750 and 1770, which show well over twice as much being shipped to the southern colonies as to New England and New York combined, where the population was much greater.

In the north, distinct regional characteristics developed, due in part to the great distances between the major centers and in part also to historical factors. New York, originally New Amsterdam, was a Dutch colony before it was ceded to the British. In the late seventeenth century, the form and ornament of its silver was directly derived from Dutch prototypes. Even in the middle of the eighteenth century, the New York silver trade was still dominated by craftsmen of Dutch extraction, and their heritage can occasionally be detected in characteristic embossed or engraved decoration. By this stage, however, form had come mainly under the influence of English taste. The two New York tankards in the collection, by Adrian Bancker and Nicholas Roosevelt (Cat. 128 and 131), both follow the standard English type of around the turn of the century. On the other hand, Boston tankards from the second quarter of the century show a distinct type of development in which the body tends to taper toward the lip, and the cover, increasingly domed,

is surmounted by a pyriform baluster finial. The tankard of about 1720 by John Coney (Cat. 127) is in this form, although the finial was probably added at a later date to make it more fashionable.

Before Independence, the taste of northern colonies remained conservative, and demand continued for certain types of plate long after they had passed out of fashion in England. The Boston spout cup (Cat. 135) was made around 1730, but would probably not have been produced in England much after the turn of the century; similarly, the porringer (Cat. 132) is not found in English silver much after the first quarter of the century but continued to be popular in New England even after Independence.

English fashions were followed much more closely in Philadelphia, which by the mid-eighteenth century was the second largest English-speaking city in the world. The leading mid-eighteenth century silversmith in Philadelphia was Joseph Richardson, who maintained close business connections with London. The bowl and salver in the Fowler collection (Cat. 130 and 141) fully justify his reputation as the most outstanding exponent of the rococo style in American silver. Richardson was also in the vanguard of the neo-classical style which spread to America soon after its adoption in England; he led the field in the production of silver based on the urn form and made relatively inexpensively from mechanically-rolled sheets of silver. The use of such machinery in the production of silver tended to favor large-scale manufacturers, since it reduced costs but at the same time required a considerable capital investment. The style is represented in the Fowler collection by a plain and a fluted urn by Paul Revere II of Boston (Cat. 133 and 134). Revere is probably the most famous of all American craftsmen because of his patriotic exploits, but he was also a highly successful entrepreneur who was well placed to respond to developments in the silver industry, since he owned both a cannon foundry and a copper rolling mill. During the nineteenth century, silver manufacture in America, as in England, became increasingly industrialized, with an inevitably negative effect on quality, until the innovative experiments in hand-wrought silver promoted by Gorham and Tiffany at the end of the century.

Detail of Paul Revere sugar urn. FMCH X87.906. *(See Cat. 133, page 110).*

127. (ABOVE, LEFT). **TANKARD.** Silver.
Boston, c. 1720, the finial probably c. 1750.

Marks: Maker's mark of John Coney (c. 1655-1722);
marked next to upper portion of handle just below rim.

Height: 21 cm (8¼"). FMCH x87.920.

128. (ABOVE, RIGHT). **TANKARD.** Silver.
New York, c. 1730.

Marks: Maker's mark of Adrian Bancker (1703-72);
marked twice at lip.
The handle is engraved with initials R over IS.

Height: 20.7cm (8"). FMCH x87.921.

129. COFFEE POT. Silver and wood. Boston, c.1745.

Marks: Maker's mark of Benjamin Burt (1729-1805); marked under base.

The underneath of the base is dated 1745 and engraved with initials C over NM and with two scratch weights (39:5 and 41:10).

Height: 28.8 cm (11¼"). FMCH x87.908.

130. BOWL. Silver. Philadelphia, c.1760.

Marks: Maker's mark of Joseph Richardson (1711-84); marked twice under base.

The bowl is engraved with a cypher of initials IA.

Diameter: 15.5 cm (6"). FMCH x87.912.

131. TANKARD. Silver.
New York, c. 1740.

Marks: Maker's mark of Nicholas Roosevelt (1715-69); marked twice at lip. The cover and the lower junction of the handle are decorated with two Louis XV silver coins, dated 1728 and 1734.

Height: 19.2 cm (7½"). FMCH X87.919.

132. PORRINGER. Silver.
Boston, c. 1800.

Marks: Maker's mark of Joseph Foster (1760-1839); marked under handle.

Width: 21.7 cm (8½"). FMCH X87.911.

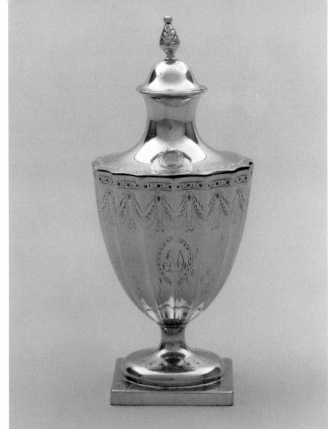

133. (ABOVE, LEFT) **SUGAR URN.** Silver.
Boston, c. 1780.

Marks: Maker's mark of Paul Revere II (1735-1818);
marked on lip.

Height: 25 cm (9¾"). FMCH X87.906.A,B.

134. (ABOVE, RIGHT) **SUGAR URN.** Silver.
Boston, c. 1790.

Marks: Maker's mark of Paul Revere II (1735-1818);
marked on foot.

Engraved with initials AD on body and cover.

Height: 23.5 cm (9¼"). FMCH X87.907.A,B.

135. COVERED SPOUT CUP. Silver.
Boston, c. 1730.

Marks: Maker's mark of Samuel Edwards (1705-62);
marked under base.

Height: 14.0 cm (5½"). FMCH X87.902.A,B.

136. COMMUNION SERVICE. Silver.

Albany, New York, c. 1816.

Marks: Maker's mark of Robert Shepherd and William Boyd; marked under bases.

The set comprises a flagon and four communion beakers (two shown); the flagon is engraved "The Church of Christ in Lenox 1816."

Height: 29.5cm (11½"). FMCH X87.1001.A-I.

137. EGG WARMER. Silver.
Boston, c. 1819.

Marks: Maker's mark of Lewis Cary (1798-1834); marked under base and under stand.

The warmer and stand are engraved on applied plaques with initials ABA, said to be those of Abigail Brooks Adams, daughter-in-law of President John Quincy Adams.

Height: 24.9 cm (9¾").

FMCH X87.918.A-C.

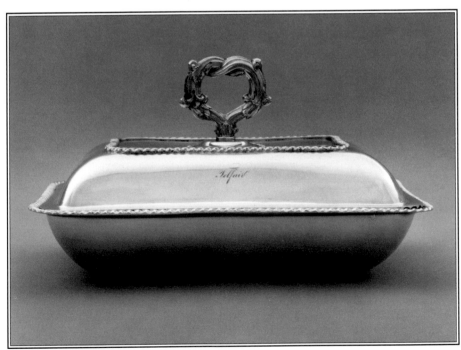

138. PAIR OF ENTRÉE DISHES.
Silver. *(One shown).*
New York, c. 1830.

Marks: Maker's mark of William Thomson (recorded c. 1810-45); marked under bases.

Width: 30.4 cm (11⅞").

FMCH X87.917.A-F.

139. PAIR OF SALVERS. Silver.
Albany, New York, c. 1840.

Marks: Maker's mark of Gerardus Boyce (c. 1795-1880), also stamped N HAYDEN CHARLESTON for the retailer; marked under rims.
Width: 25.5 cm (10"). FMCH X87.1002.A,B.

140. BEAKER. Silver and silver-gilt.
Rhode Island, c. 1800.

Marks: Maker's mark of David Vinton; marked three times under base.
Heraldry: The crest is unidentified.
Height: 10.2 cm (4"). FMCH X87.1004.

141. SALVER. Silver.

Philadelphia, c. 1760.

Marks: Maker's mark of Joseph Richardson (1711-84);
marked on upper surface.

Diameter: 40.9cm (16"). FMCH X87.913.

REFERENCES CITED

Barr, Elaine

1980   *George Wickes 1698-1761 Royal Goldsmith.*
        London: Studio Vista.

Belden, Louise Conway

1980   *Marks of American Silversmiths in the Ineson-Bissell
        Collection.*
        Charlottesville: University Press of Virginia.

Beuque, Émile

1925-28 *Dictionnaire des Poinçons Officiels Français et Étrangers.*
        Paris.

Clayton, Michael

1985   *The Collector's Dictionary of the Silver and Gold
        of Great Britain and North America.*
        Second edition. London: Antique Collector's Club.

Culme, John

1987   *The Directory of Gold and Silversmiths, Jewellers
        and Allied Traders 1838-1914.*
        Woodbridge: Antique Collectors' Club. 2 volumes.

Goldberg, T.G., and M.M. Postnikova-Loseva

n.d.   "Kleimenie Serevrianykh izdelii v xviii vv" (Marking
        of silver objects in the 17th and early 18th centuries),
        *Trudy G.I.M. (Transactions of the State Historical
        Museum, Moscow).* Moscow.

Grimwade, Arthur

1976   *London Goldsmiths 1697-1837, Their Marks and Lives.*
        London: Faber and Faber.

Hayward, J.F.

1976   *Virtuoso Goldsmiths and the Triumph of Mannerism 1540-1620.*
        London: Sotheby Parke Bernet Pubs. Ltd.

Jackson, Charles James

1921   *English Goldsmiths and their Marks: A History of the Gold-
        smiths and Plate Workers of England, Scotland and Ireland.*
        Second edition, revised and enlarged.
        London: Macmillan and Company.
        Reprint, New York: Dover Publications, 1964.

Oman, Charles

1978   *English Engraved Silver 1150 to 1900.*
        London: Faber and Faber.

Rosenberg, Marc

1922   *Der Goldschmiede Merkzeichen.*
        Third edition.
        Frankfurt. 4 volumes.

Scheffler, Wolfgang

1965   *Goldschmiede Niedersachsens.*
        Berlin: Walter de Gruyter. 2 volumes.

Schliemann, Erich

1985   *Die Goldschmiede Hamburgs.*
        Hamburg: Verlag Schliemann. 3 volumes.

Schroder, Timothy

1988a   *The Gilbert Collection of Gold and Silver.*
        Los Angeles: Los Angeles County Museum of Art.

1988b   *The National Trust Book of English Domestic Silver,
        1500-1900.*
        Harmondsworth: Viking in association with
        The National Trust.

Seling, Helmut

1980   *Die Kunst der Augsburger Goldschmiede 1529-1868.*
        Munich: Verlag C.H. Beck. 3 volumes.

PUBLICATION PRESENTATION

Daniel R. Brauer — *Design*
Henrietta Cosentino — *Editing*
Denis J. Nervig — *Photography*
Patrick Dowdey — *Editorial Assistance*

*Typesetting and layout were accomplished
by the Editor and the Designer on Macintosh computers
using Aldus PageMaker 4.01
and Adobe Garamond font software.*